Milestones
in American
Literary History

CONTRIBUTIONS IN AMERICAN STUDIES

SERIES EDITOR **Robert H. Walker**

Milestones in American Literary History

Robert E. Spiller

Foreword by Robert H. Walker

Contributions in American Studies, Number 27

GREENWOOD PRESS
Westport, Connecticut • London, England

Library of Congress Cataloging in Publication Data

Spiller, Robert Ernest, 1896-
  Milestones in American literary history.

  (Contributions in American studies ; no. 27)
  Includes index.
  1. American literature—History and criticism—Collected works.
2. Criticism—United States.
I. Title.
PS121.S56   810'.9   76-47170
ISBN 0-8371-9403-2

Library of Congress Catalog Card Number: 76-47170
ISBN: 0-8371-9403-2

 First published in 1977

Greenwood Press, Inc.
51 Riverside Avenue, Westport, Connecticut 06880

Printed in the United States of America

❧ CONTENTS ❧

✒ FOREWORD ✒

The center of this collection is the *Literary History of the United States* (LHUS), first published in November 1948.[1] Its central value is in the opportunity it provides for understanding and assessing the philosophy which unifies the LHUS, that landmark statement of America's meaning.

The contents of this collection are neither blindly inclusive nor casually selective. Their first element is a body of reviews, thirty-two in number, dating from a 1922 response to a Lewis Mumford work and ending with a 1960 appraisal of Willard Thorp's critique of twentieth-century American literature. Chosen from a much larger available number, these particular reviews build deliberately toward a major philosophy as expressed in the editions of LHUS through the "definitive" one of 1963. Although the scope of these reviews is broad, they do not constitute a series of unrelated perceptions, however valuable in its own way such an inclusive compendium might have been. Rather, they retain a tight focus. Their responses to the major interpretations of American literature during four decades show both the evolution of an original idea and, simultaneously, the relation of LHUS to the important literary philosophies of the day.

The epilogue consists of two prefaces: an open letter to literary historians and a personal account of long and complicated discus-

---

1. *Literary History of the United States,* edited by Robert E. Spiller, Willard Thorp, Thomas H. Johnson, and Henry S. Canby. 3 vols. New York: The Macmillan Company, 1948, 1953, 1963, 1974.

sions and decisions that finally led to the remarkable fusion of effort that was the LHUS. This is not only the story of philosophical evolution but the social and political history of a cultural event complete with names, dates, and places. If the LHUS itself is history, then these four extended essays constitute its historiography.

The third element in the collection, while perfectly visible, will not strike all readers with appropriate force. This third element is time. It manifests itself in a complete set of headnotes, composed by Robert Spiller in 1976 while looking over his own shoulder as far back as fifty-four years. This perspective reveals both a crucial development in point of view and a set of remarkable consistencies diligently guarded.

More important, this time element allows for the consideration of a statement echoed so often in these pages that it becomes a coda. It opens the 1948 LHUS preface: "Each generation should produce at least one literary history of the United States, for each generation must define the past in its own terms." But that was 1948 and we are now sliding toward the 1980s. Where is the new literary statement for that generation, which has seemed so exceptionally committed to throwing out the past and trusting no one born before 1948? Is the answer, perhaps implied in Robert Spiller's letter to Walter Blair, that the LHUS so acutely anticipated literary trends that an abnormal life span was assured? Is it that the LHUS in 1948 represented the crest of a long-building tidal wave of American cultural assertion followed by an age so notably less confident that a true successor could hardly be expected? Are there other answers that would emerge more from a close technical examination of the literary-historical architect, his craftsmen and his building materials, to use that metaphor which permeates this collection as surely as the generational coda sets its tone?

For many readers, these analytical questions will await the nostalgic joys of immersion in those heady literary scenes of the 1920s and 1930s with their rich and almost daily triumphs recalled by such names as Robert Frost, T. S. Eliot, William Faulkner, Ezra Pound, Ernest Hemingway, William Carlos Williams, and Eugene O'Neill. There is no need to detail this sudden wealth of imaginative outpouring; but it is important to be reminded that as American poetry and fiction and drama were finding new and flattering levels of acceptance throughout the world, so a new generation of critics and historians began to assert—for their own ever-widening audience—that American letters could no longer be perceived as a pale, colonial reflection of some mother lode. If American writers could not be written off as apprentices to European masters, then their achievements needed to be categorized in some other way.

It is a principal joy as well as an essential justification of this collection that as these new literary viewpoints emerged, Robert Spiller was chosen to review them with an incredible regularity. It was as though the book review editors were deliberately grooming this man for his eventual task. His readers, then and now, may claim a reward that is valuable for separate perceptions and for cumulative impact.

The review is, to be sure, a literary form itself; but for Robert Spiller it is less a form of art than an aspect of reporting. The book itself is the news, he has said. To function becomingly, the reporter will "understand, identify, and interpret," leaving evaluation to the critic who follows. If this is a simple definition, it by no means defines a simple act; for, years after the appearance of these reviews, readers are still aiming for understandings superior to those supplied by Spiller to the works of Parrington and Mumford, Rourke and Brooks, Gabriel, Matthiessen, and the rest.

To recall the works covered by these reviews is to be reminded that the critical pattern of this era was not so neatly bifurcated as some like to make it: a square of Marxists on the left, a forum of New Humanists on the right, and only the author's sweet reason in between. There were, in fact, many more distinguishable persuasions, as well as shades of attitude within each. Vernon L. Parrington, for example, is often made to stand rather starkly for those who would see literature against a social and political background. But he was joined in this general predilection by others as various as Lewis Mumford, Howard Mumford Jones, Percy H. Boynton, and Alfred Kazin. And there was also emerging a new kind of cultural identity for literature as seen in the work of Constance Rourke.

The New Humanism had its impact (best seen in the review of Norman Foerster's *Towards Standards*), but there were other definitions of classicism ranging from Randall Stewart's preoccupation with Old Testament fundamentalism to Henry S. Canby's archetypes of nativism. No two of these positions were alike. For the man designing a generation's statement, each had utility, none could be allowed to dominate.

Two of the major complexities of the time were the New Criticism and Freudian criticism. On the surface, both would seem quite inimical to the historian who saw the primary value of literature in its reflection of a total culture. Although LHUS embraced neither of these views, each had its effect.

The New Criticism, near its zenith when LHUS was published, often seemed grandly intolerant of all historical judgments on literature. Robert Spiller and his colleagues chose not to respond in kind but to study, use, adapt, and benefit. The New Criticism, wrote Spiller, had helped the cultural historian by placing stress on the literary product as opposed to the personal act of creation. Freed from the tyranny of biographical minutiae, the interpreter could use new critical perceptions to focus on cultural as well as formal meanings. Thus a leading New Critic, Richard P. Blackmur, could write a pivotal chapter on Henry James without at all destroying the unities of the LHUS.

Spiller's reaction to D. H. Lawrence's *Studies in Classic American Literature* accurately mirrors the general unfriendliness of the LHUS group toward critiques stressing complexes and neuroses. Joseph Wood Krutch, who wrote two chapters for LHUS, also wrote one of the early Freudian studies of Edgar Allen Poe. In humorous retreat from his early enthusiasms, Krutch was fond of recounting how it finally occurred to him that the crucial problem was not to demonstrate Poe's kinship to Oedipus but to explain why others, similarly disturbed, had failed to produce a ''Raven.'' Thus Krutch, Spiller, and the other LHUS contributors not only eschewed psycholiterary readings but tended to deemphasize literary works dominated by Freudian motifs (like some by Sherwood Anderson and Robinson Jeffers).

Yet aspects of the Freudian approach were beginning to penetrate the LHUS by way of a rather complex evolution. The line of descent included Parrington's political symbols as well as Rourke's cultural values. The use of images and symbols in historical work acquired justification from Freud's own somewhat self-contradictory speculation that symbols identifiable in expressions of the human unconscious were derived from the culture and varied from culture to culture. To Freudian justification was added the New Critical method of exegesis and close reading, essential to bringing forth important levels of literary meaning. This ancestry produced a movement loosely christened the "myth and symbol school." No single work was more important to its early life than *Virgin Land: The American West as Symbol and Myth* by Henry Nash Smith who, by no means incidentally, had contributed four chapters to LHUS.

The remarkable way in which LHUS made appropriate use of that wide yet delicately shaded spectrum of contemporary literary philosophies comes clearly into focus as one peruses this collection in its chronological order. In fact these many philosophies were adapted with such sensitivity that the LHUS became—quite understandably in retrospect—not just a recasting of the cultural past but a kind of prophecy of the literary future.

Looking against the chronological grain, however, gives a different cast to the forty years covered by this collection. For whatever their political or philosophical coloration, the books and the reviews combine to express an exuberant confidence in American literature as a subject worthy of the world's concern. Foreign and native critics might dispute the relative worth of Poe and Fitzgerald, the relative artistry of Frost and Eliot, but no one seemed to doubt that American letters had earned their passport and visa as one of the rising world power's more substantial exports. Most of the LHUS writers began their professional lives under instruction that American literature was but a minor branch of a European subject, the literature of England, importantly different in no way. One can see in these pages that apologies gave way to explanations, explanations to ideas of order, and categories to a kind of imperial statement attesting to a full domain of creativity and criticism.

The 1920s and 1930s dealt with debunking and cynicism, protest and exile. Yet these years also saw a kind of straight line development in the emerging cultural self-confidence of a nation that had been the victim of its own longstanding sense of inferiority. If we look backward from the days of disillusionment following Vietnam and Watergate, the grand assurance that underlay the LHUS seems to represent an emotion that can only come once in the process of national, cultural maturity.

Although the title of this collection suggests the many works along the way that led to the LHUS, it refers mainly to the epilogue and the LHUS itself. The LHUS was indeed a milestone for literary historians whether they accepted it totally, partially, or not at all. The collected reviews help understand just how this milestone was achieved, not by avoiding divergent views but by employing them. The epilogue further shows exactly how the LHUS can be appreciated—not as a symposium of random attitudes but as a single statement with strong underlying themes and a common ground of recurring understandings that go to the core of American culture. LHUS made a statement for a generation in a way that allowed for the discovery—in the very act of its creation—of a common denominator among points of view that ranged from determined Marxism to the floating unities of the New Criticism. This statement resulted not so much from dissolving the differences as asking what their sum might be.

As chairman of the editorial board of LHUS, Robert Spiller received considerable help, which he has carefully acknowledged again in this collection. Yet it was he who sat at the table's head. It is he who must be called the work's chief designer. And so this collection also becomes the story of an individual journey that began with a "dissatisfaction with the way American literary history had until then [1928] been written, with little or no reference to its roots in the American cultural tradition. . . ." Spiller saw the publication by Van Wyck Brooks in 1915 of *America's Coming of Age* as the announcement of a challenge to those who would increase literary and cultural perceptions by uniting the two searches. The subsequent publication of the *Cambridge History of American Literature* (1917-1921) was not a satisfactory response to this challenge but made more obvious the need for a true literary historian, which Fred Lewis Pattee further defined in the June 1924 *American Mercury*.

Many scholars and critics—including Brooks and Pattee themselves—arose in answer to this call. Their contributions are strongly reflected in this collection. The full measure of Spiller's influence, in spite of his central role in the LHUS, has been harder to gauge; for he has that knack—traceable to Socrates, cultivated by Franklin, fully mature in Emerson (all friends of Robert Spiller)—of imparting ideas in such a way that the recipient often thinks them his own. A happy victim of this ruse myself, I have full room to wonder what generalizations arrived at in these introductory paragraphs are truly my own and which may have been thrown my way with deceptive innocence by this man whom I have been fortunate enough to hear in lecture hall and seminar, in living room and meeting room, and even as the director of my own first serious research.

We will likely take too much credit for what we learn from these reviews and histories, prefaces, and headnotes. If so, we will doubly please their author. The best thing about this collection is that it was collected by Robert Spiller; the best thing about its prose is that—in its concise and exact way—it is Spiller on Spiller.

ROBERT H. WALKER
April 1976

✨ACKNOWLEDGMENTS ✨

These reviews would not have been possible without the friendly cooperation of the literary editors of the journals in which they first appeared, particularly Walter Yust of the Philadelphia *Public Ledger,* Henry Seidel Canby of the *Saturday Review of Literature,* and Jay B. Hubbell and Clarence Gohdes of *American Literature.* I am also indebted to Robert H. Walker and Robert F. Lucid who encouraged me to believe that these reviews, if brought together, might tell a story and make a book.

I am indebted to the following for permission to reprint my reviews and essays, which first appeared in their pages:

American Literature, published by Duke University Press (reviews 12, 16, 17, 18, 19, 20, 21, 23, and 29).

New York Times Book Review, © 1958/1960 by The New York Times Company. Reprinted by permission. (reviews 31 and 32).

Saturday Review, successor to *Saturday Review of Literature* (reviews 6, 8, 9, 17, 24, 25, 27, 28, and 30).

Philadelphia *Inquirer,* successor to Philadelphia *Public Ledger* (reviews 1, 2, 3, 4, 7, and 10).

Macmillan Publishing Company, Inc., for prefaces to *Literary History of the United States* and *The Cycle of American Literature* and for "A Letter to American Literary Historians" from *The Third Dimension* (1965).

Pennsylvania Magazine of History and Biography (review 14).

Modern Language Association of America, for "History of a History: The Story behind *Literary History of the United States.*"

National Council of Teachers of English, publishers of *The English Journal* and *College English* (reviews 5 and 22).

Journal of English and Germanic Philology, published by the University of Illinois Press (review 15).

American Quarterly, published by the University of Pennsylvania (review 13).

ABOUT THE AUTHOR

Robert E. Spiller is Felix E. Schelling Professor Emeritus of English at the University of Pennsylvania and a founding president of the American Studies Association. Among his other works are *Fenimore Cooper, Critic of His Times, The Early Lectures of Ralph Waldo Emerson, The Cycle of American Literature,* and *The Third Dimension.*

Milestones
in American
Literary History

1

1923

THE STORY OF UTOPIAS
by Lewis Mumford

In the early 1920s, Lewis Mumford was one of the group of freelance critics of society and literature that clustered for the moment around Van Wyck Brooks and contributed fairly regularly to the *Freeman* and the *Dial*. This, his first book, aided my search for insights and values more than I realized at that time. Although it does not deal specifically with the American dream, it provides a wide historical perspective for any study of man's efforts to create a living society from the pattern of his ideals. The hope that I express in the final sentence of my review was richly fulfilled by Mumford's lifetime of imaginative explorations over the whole range of American and world cultures through the media of literature, architecture, urban planning, human history, and the thought of the humanistic philosophers of all time. To have identified the concept of utopia as the mainspring of the life work of one of our great humanists at the start of his career was a prediction that was richly rewarded by a shelf of cultural histories culminating in *The Myth of the Machine* (1967, 1970).

The sincere doctor is willing, should the need arise, to take his own medicine, the sincere preacher lives according to his precept insofar as he is able, and Lewis Mumford has written in his *Story of Utopias* a very successful embodiment of the social theory for which he argues with much of the zest of the martyrs of other days.

New York: Boni and Liveright, 1922. Reviewed in Philadelphia *Public Ledger*, January 1923.

The Story of Utopias is introduced by an analysis of the author's viewpoint in a preface which expands into a chapter. It is his intention to write the other half of the story of mankind. His friend, Mr. Van Loon, had already written with paternal explicitness and simplicity the long and fascinating story of the world that was and is; it remained to write the equally fascinating story of the world that is not and ought to be. It is a laudable ambition; the unlocking for the multitude of the vast treasure chest of knowledge and of dreams heretofore accessible only to the chosen few who had the magic key of learning. We are to be taken by the hand and gently led into unknown realms where we would be amazed and lost without this guidance. For this Mr. Mumford is admirably equipped. He has a keen discerning mind, has read widely within and outside his field and has at all times kept his head serenely above the battle, seeing and interpreting always in the light of an absorbing ideal. He tells us to look for two sorts of utopias, that of escape and that of reconstruction, and he sharpens our wits for a battle with ideas which might otherwise prove dry and uninteresting.

It is in the body of the book that we see most clearly the merits of this altogether unscholarly but highly enlightening point of view. Matthew Arnold, with his Victorian propriety and wisdom, once demanded that criticism not only propagate the best that is known and thought in the world but that it be disinterested. Mr. Mumford is interested with the spirited eagerness of the reformer, almost to the point of prejudice. Under the banner of his own idea he leads into the battle. The result is a survey of men's social dreams from Plato to H. G. Wells that strikes fire from the flint of dead ideas on almost every page, but which selects utopias and selects from utopias as arbitrarily as a draft board. It is not so much what men have thought and dreamed as what Mr. Mumford thinks of it all that gives the survey its value.

By the time we reach Mr. Wells and his *Modern Utopia* the author's impatience to launch his own social theories infects the blood, and the kettle-drums and trombones swing into a sweeping and overwhelming climax. This is what we have been waiting for. The Country House, symbolic of the landed and idle gentry of today, is torn from its foundations; Coketown, with its dirty factories and slaves at work, is blasted; and Megalopolis, the capital of the National State, rocks on its foundations. Here is the masterstroke of the whole book. The philosophy of paper is a metaphorical condemnation of the roots of society, their pious uniformity and soulless hypocrisy, as awakening and challenging as the still fierce voice of Carlyle's philosophy of clothes. If the book were written only for this, it were [*sic*] worth the reading.

But it is written for more. It is written to lay the foundations of a new *eu*topia, a *eu*topia in which half-worlds go and we build horizontally in the light of universal principles and not vertically in the light of special interests and privileges. And it is here that Mr. Mumford swallows his own medicine and stands before the world as his own symbol of health. All true science and all true art is and must be propaganda: that is, they must exist for ends only beyond themselves, ends which shape and construct and not merely investigate or destroy. The new social order must take into account "the immediate diversity and complexity of man's environment" and create a "vivid pattern that would move men to great things." Mr. Mumford is in the mood to write a utopia of his own after he has laid such foundations, and one cannot help wishing that he would.

2

1923

STUDIES IN CLASSIC AMERICAN LITERATURE
by D. H. Lawrence

No one was prepared for the sudden assault by the English novelist D. H. Lawrence on the established images of America's major literary figures, and most of us found ourselves on the other side of the fence. Approaching literature from the angle of the then new-depth psychology, he read our classics not for what they said or how well they were written but for what they revealed of the hidden lives of their authors and their culture. The result was a major critical work that has profoundly influenced the course of American literary history ever since; but my own reactions at the time were, as will be apparent, mixed.

"Little children, it is the last time . . . even now there are many anti-Christs," said the Apostle John many years ago. Antichrist has taken many forms, but never before has he appeared as a critic of American literature. D. H. Lawrence is just the sort of materialist that the Apostle, were he living today, would probably warn most vehemently against. And he in turn has little use for the Apostle. "He wasn't named John for nothing," says Lawrence in speaking of the "long-nosed salvationist," the Swede who interfered in a much-deserved whipping in Dana's *Two Years Before the Mast*. The

---

New York: Thomas Seltzer, 1923. Reviewed in Philadelphia *Public Ledger,* November 17, 1923.

scorn which John would probably feel for this 'worshiper of the dark soul of man is amply repaid by the undisguised hatred of Lawrence for the salvationist, the idealist with his "wet hanky" for the sins of the world.

"The Father had His day, and fell."—Judaism

"The Son had his day, and fell."—Christianity

"It is the day of the Holy Ghost."—Psycho-analysis.

This is the philosophy behind these studies. "The whole Sermon on the Mount becomes a litany of white vice." White vice? Can vice be white? Yes, if the soul is verily "a dark forest" in which "gods, strange gods, come forth from the forest into the clearing of my known self, and then go back," and if I, mankind, must "try always to recognize and submit to the gods in me and the gods in other men and women."

This is not the place to criticize the religion of a critic. It is the place to try to understand it in order that his criticism may not be confused by our false conceptions of his basic beliefs. The author of this work on American literature does not believe in the basic tenets of Christianity. But Christianity weathered the storm of evolution and rather profited by it in the end; perhaps it may weather the storm of this dark forest in which the soul is running after its strange gods and shaking them by the hand and then passing them on in the darkness. We may think what we like of it as a religion. As a point of view it is one of the most stimulating things that have come into literary criticism for a long time. Even Mencken or Macy seems like a pedant and an academician when Lawrence is making the sparks fly. The display of verbal fireworks is breath-taking.

This book is not a condemnation of American authors, either classic or modern. It is a totally new evaluation of the old literature of America, which sails in a most astounding way past the most modern main-streety sort of thing, and attains its sense of novelty by reaching old harbors in totally new channels. It is nothing new to say that Ben Franklin was a lusty old hypocrite, that Cooper was a romanticist in literature and a bear in life, that Poe was a psycho-pathic phenomenon, that Hawthorne was a dreamer who dreamed more than he knew, and that Whitman caught the essence of American democracy and gave it soul, even though that soul had something of the fixity and form of putty. These are the things that the driest of students of American literature have been expounding in discourses and hammering over desks for at least a decade, if not longer. It does not seem so horribly radical when we look at it from that point of view. It seems rather tame and conservative and more likely to arouse protest from modernists like Masters and Sherwood Anderson than from the reverencers of the old. In fact, we can be thankful to this Englishman for taking us back to our elder masters and showing us that, after all, our national consciousness is as much Anglo-Saxon as it is Russian or Irish or anything else. The soul of Crèvecoeur, French though it was, could struggle, even in its high heels, to the then rugged American wilderness and meet that of the proud English Cooper, with his false democracy shorn from him, in a free forest. There is something in these old fellows, something that we may have been inclined to overlook. If they do nothing else, they at least suggest that the melting pot always has been and still is melting. Fortunately, it has turned out as yet no soul which may be stamped "Made in America" and sent out into the world with a self-starter and a spare tire and the blessings of our "national consciousness" upon it.

Granting Lawrence's bias, his desire to read all life and all artists in terms of his own psycho-analytical mind, we find his comparative estimate of American authors to be sane, well-proportioned and refreshingly conservative. Questioning his philosophical basis, we are lost in a labyrinth of controversy. It is safest to take the book for what it is, to revel in the brilliancy of its incomparable wit and keen judgment, and then, if our consciences say nay, to throw it gently into the fire.

3

1927

✣ MAIN CURRENTS ✣
IN AMERICAN THOUGHT
by Vernon Louis Parrington

Volume I: *The Colonial Mind, 1620-1800*
Volume II: *The Romantic Revolution in America, 1800-1860*

The first two volumes of *Main Currents in American Thought*
exploded unannounced upon the scene of American literary
scholarship in 1927. Its author, Vernon L. Parrington of the
University of Washington, was then virtually unknown—at
least in the East—and his book, which he had thought was to
be a history of American literature, was retitled by his publisher as an intellectual and cultural history, which it mainly
was. But the younger scholars in American literature who
were already deserting the field of English literature with its
marriage to Anglo-Saxon philology immediately recognized
it as an invitation to join forces with the new and progressive
scholarship in American history represented by such innova-
tors as Turner, Beard, and Becker. The die was cast.

Among the many recent surveys of American civilization in terms
of her history, her literature, her architecture and various other
avenues of her national development, Prof. Parrington's study
takes its place as one of the most scholarly and most original. His

---

New York: Harcourt, Brace and Co., 1927. Reviewed in Philadelphia *Public Ledger*
May 14, 1927.

approach to his subject is radical, although there are already many
who agree with it; his method is that of the scholar who seeks first
sources in every possible instance rather than being willing to rely
on the findings of others. Primarily a study of American literature,
his book leads to conclusions more strictly in the fields of politics,
history and philosophy. With esthetic excellences he has almost no
concern. Literature is to him merely a convenient vehicle for the
expression of all thought and experience. His efforts are directed
toward tracing the main avenues of a national thought from its
earliest days; the forms of expression of that thought are admittedly
secondary.

His thesis is briefly this: America inherited from the past of Europe certain bequests out of which she shaped her distinctive civilization. The most important of these were the English independency
which found its chief expression in Puritanism; French romantic
theory, which is here defined in economic rather than literary terms
and is essentially the doctrine of the French Revolution; and a miscellaneous group of English and Continental movements of the
nineteenth century, notably a laissez-faire political economy resultant from the industrial revolution, the impulse of scientific discovery and various theories of collectivism. These last are apparently
to be grouped for the third volume under the head: "The Beginnings of Critical Realism in America." The influences of the first
two are studied each in a separate volume, already published.

The result of this review of our literature in economic and social
terms is somewhat startling. It leads to a realignment of names, a
subordination of some writers whom we have been taught to regard
as of the first rank, a degree of emphasis for some others whom we
have hardly noticed, and an entirely new basis for our estimates of
many of the unquestioned great. It relieves us from the necessity of
considering Michael Wigglesworth as a poet and gives us a new
insight into such figures as Franklin, Jefferson, Brackenridge,
Hopkinson, Freneau and even such old Puritans as John Cotton,
the Mathers and John Wise. In a slightly later period—the twenties
and thirties of the last century—however, the new attitude, although
still enlightening, is not so completely satisfying. Such men as Emerson, Cooper and Irving have unquestioned right to first rank as
literary as well as social figures. But we have certainly tended to

overemphasize their fiction, their poetry and their literary essays, in which they derived perhaps too generously from English literature of the previous century, and the newer view of their ideas as social criticism is helpful to a fuller understanding of both them and their times. Particularly is this true of Cooper, the genuine value of whose social criticism has been ignored because it blocked his career as a romantic novelist, "The American Scott."

It will be interesting to see to what conclusions Dr. Parrington's third volume will lead him. His basis of judgment is the most reasonable one of all for the period of his first; it startles us into attention in his second, but leaves us with the feeling that he has emphasized the neglected rather than the most important aspect of our thought; in the third, which covers the period of our awakening into more truly native art-consciousness, his view will probably be less satisfying, and he will be more definitely tempted to radical extremes. Thus far every word in his two volumes must be given serious attention, and his work may be viewed as a rather specialized history of our literature and an illuminating survey of our social evolution, stimulating because of both its thoroughness and its novelty.

4

1927

❧ A HISTORY OF ❧ ENGLISH LITERATURE
by Emile Legouis and Louis Cazamian[1]

❧ THE REVOLUTIONARY SPIRIT ❧ IN FRANCE AND AMERICA
by Bernard Fäy[2]

At first glance, a new history of English literature written by two French professors at the Sorbonne is not especially relevant to the present inquiry. I was probably attracted to it because, with my principal training in English rather than American literature, I could see it as a revolt against the established point of view toward English literary history and therefore as a preliminary to the kind of attack I instinctively felt was coming.

In breaking away from the classical studies, the pioneers of English literary study who founded the Modern Language Association at the close of the nineteenth century turned to the Indo-Teutonic origins and languages as a substitute for Latin and Greek, and any revolt against the concept of English as a basically Anglo-Saxon literature was by 1920 a heresy in its turn. Professors Legouis and Cazamian recognized cor-

---

1. Translated by W. D. Macinnes and the authors, 2 vols. New York: The Macmillan Company, 1927.
2. Translated by Ramon Guthrie. New York: Harcourt, Brace and Co., 1927. Reviewed in Philadelphia *Public Ledger,* December 17, 1927.

rectly that the middle period in English literary history could hardly be distinguished from the French of the same period in theme, mode, and form. Furthermore Cazamian was one of the first to turn away from the linguistic discipline and to measure the historical course of a literature against its own social and intellectual backgrounds. This book is central to my own story because it laid much of the theoretical groundwork for the revolt of my generation of American literary historians.

Bernard Fäy, who later wrote a life of Benjamin Franklin and then came to an unhappy end as a collaborator with the invaders in World War II, in this book made a useful contribution to intellectual history by his study of the international flow of political ideas. American scholars were also beginning to think along these lines.

Before the late war, American scholarship turned for inspiration and guidance to the great philological and historical scholars of Germany. France had contributed great scholars likewise, but in no such numbers as her neighbor. For the one great philologist, Gaston Paris, to whom she could point, Germany could count dozens, from the time of Grimm to the then present. But the war brought about a change. Germany had no longer the economic surplus which is essential to such a luxury as scholarship, and the eyes of the English-speaking world were turned elsewhere. France immediately made every effort to fill the gap, as is witnessed by a compilation entitled, "Science and Learning in France," assembled by American scholars and published by the Society for American Fellowships in French Universities in 1917.

Ten years have passed since this propaganda was undertaken, and we find some surprising results. The Sorbonne now has a department of American culture (literature and history) under the capable headship of Prof. Cestre, and the list of French works on English and American history and literature is constantly growing. But the effect of the movement is rather the contrary of that which was intended. American students and scholars are, doubtless, seeking out the French universities in increasing numbers; but a more significant fact is the attention of French scholars which has been turned to the materials of Anglo-Saxon culture. We (and England may consider herself with us in this matter) are being scrutinized by our ally of the last war. What scrutiny will eventually bring forth is yet to be determined, but the two books here presented form notable indexes to what we may expect.

One fact we may note. The French genius is rather for survey investigations than for detailed and analytic studies such as attracted the Germans. The result is an emphasis on the relationship of literature to political and social history instead of a scientific analysis of the language structure of literary work. Both of these books are significant and comprehensive historical estimates of foreign cultures, the one in terms of literature, the other in terms of political history. Naturally enough also, they emphasize our historical connections with the French; the importance of the Anglo-Norman period in English literature (Legouis), the origins of American revolutionary ideals in the French philosophic thought of the period (Fäy) and French sources for both classicism and romanticism (Cazamian). But such emphasis is useful in readjusting our more or less conventionalized theories about our past. We have been too meticulous in tracing the Teutonic origins of our culture, whereas the romance nations brought us, among other things, the Renaissance and Rousseauism, two of the foundation stones of our present-day thought.

It is impossible to discuss here the detailed contributions of these books. They will sound strange and inaccurate to many who are accustomed to other lines of thought, but their strangeness is distinctly a recommendation, and their seeming inaccuracy more a seeming than a being. These men have treated their sources with the care and conscience of the best of scholars. M. Legouis and M. Cazamian tell an old story with the freshness of a new approach, and M. Fäy tells virtually a new story, so much have his investigations contributed to our knowledge.

5

1928

✣ THE REINTERPRETATION OF ✣ AMERICAN LITERATURE: SOME CONTRIBUTIONS TOWARD THE UNDERSTANDING OF ITS HISTORICAL DEVELOPMENT
edited by Norman Foerster

By 1920 the Modern Language Association of America was willing to admit that there was such a thing as American literature, and the first meeting of a special study group devoted to that subject was held at the annual convention in December. The first three years of this group were somewhat uncertain, but by 1924 it had achieved an identity and was taking inventory of the philosophy and the resources of American literary study. *The Reinterpretation of American Literature* was the first fruit of that growing sense of community and mission. It reprinted F. L. Pattee's *American Mercury* essay, "A Call for a Literary Historian," and printed for the first time, as an introduction, Norman Foerster's definitive statement of the uniqueness of American literature in the modern world. "The culture out of which it first issued was not a native growth but a highly elaborate culture transplanted to a wilderness that receded slowly as the frontier was pushed westward." Providing a professional Declaration of Independence for the new discipline, this book laid the foundations for the quarterly *American Literature,* which began publication the following year. My review was my first to appear in the *English Journal* and was directed primarily to the secondary-school teacher.

New York: Harcourt, Brace and Co., 1928. Reviewed in *English Journal* 18 (September 1929): 609-610.

This book is at once a challenge and a reply. In recent years the
historian of America has completely revised the traditional con-
ception of our nation's past. Myths have been dispelled and forces
distinctively American, such as the westward movement of the
frontier, have been assigned their just place in the chronicle of past
events. Our knowledge of American history today approximates
that degree of logic and accuracy which is the ideal of the scientific
historian.

Parallel with this change of attitude there has been developing
among students of all literatures a tendency to explain forms and
movements in literary history by more scientific formulae than
those of divine inspiration or even linguistic evolution. Social, economic, and philosophical factors have received more careful study
in an effort to discover their effects upon the writings of nations,
periods, or individual authors.

The essays of Professors Pattee, Foerster, Schlesinger, and Clark
reflect these tendencies. In a sense, Mr. Pattee issues the challenge
in his "Call for a Literary Historian," and the other three reply
that they are quite ready to discard the worn-out and meaningless
classification of our literature by periods, and to substitute for it an
interpretation in terms of social and economic factors, as well as of
such philosophical movements as romanticism and realism. The
final essay of Mr. Clark is to be especially commended for its sane
and balanced judgment. Fully recognizing the claims of the new
school of thought, it calls attention also to the excellences of the old
and demonstrates in a very practical manner how the teacher may
profit by the best in both attitudes.

In elaboration of special aspects of the new approach the chapters
on the interdependence of American and European literatures by
Howard Mumford Jones and that on the recent realistic movement
in the novel by V. L. Parrington are the most successful. Both obviously are summaries of the anticipated final volumes of their respective analyses of American thought, and both reflect much sound
scholarship and original thinking. The review of the frontier movement by Jay B. Hubbell and that of romanticism in America by
Paul Kauffman are less satisfactory, largely because of the difficulty
of defining these two factors and a commendable fear of dogmatism
on the part of both authors. The bibliographies of Gregory L. Paine
and Ernest E. Leisy are useful.

The weakness of the volume is that common to all such compilations, the inconsistencies and inequalities naturally resulting from the partnership of minds in agreement only on fundamental principles. But if it succeeds in provoking the teacher in elementary school, in high school, and in college, as well as the student of obscure sources, to approach our national literature in a more critical and scientific spirit than formerly, it will have served its principal purpose. The myth of Washington's cherry tree gives promise of an early and graceful retirement from school texts of American history; let us hope that we may soon learn to look upon Longfellow as something less than a god and Whitman as something more than an old villain.

6

1928

✧ AMERICA AND FRENCH CULTURE ✧
1750-1848
by Howard Mumford Jones

In the first sentence of his essay, "The European Background," in the reinterpretation volume, Howard Mumford Jones states bluntly the proposition to which he was to devote the major energies of a lifetime: "American literature belongs to the great family of west-European literatures." It was he more than anyone else who gave the new movement a positive meaning. Instead of being a revolt against the narrow English orientation, it could now be seen as a part of the spread of the Renaissance over the Western world. The book here reviewed gives little evidence of the sweep of his philosophical understanding of the case; it was rather the exhaustive exploration of the facts underlying his generalization. With this sort of foundation he could speak with the authority of sound scholarship—which he does in a later essay in this volume.

The survey of a culture over a period of one hundred years is a difficult task under any circumstances, especially when that culture is to be studied in terms of its many and varied manifestations rather than merely of its general principles. Dr. Jones has undertaken an even more difficult problem, for in the study of a foreign influence, both that influence and the civilization affected by it must have some sort of preliminary definition or analysis.

Chapel Hill: The University of North Carolina Press, 1928. Reviewed in *Saturday Review of Literature* 5 (July 28, 1928): 8.

The most significant aspect of his work is his statement of his method of approach to this complex problem. There has recently been an increasing tendency among American literary historians to reject the older method of the study of writers and their works in convenient geographical and esthetic groups, chronologically arranged. Instead, literature is to be taken as merely one of many avenues toward an understanding of civilization. Thus, in the work of Parrington, Rusk, and others, social forces receive an extensive consideration, but they are still secondary to their own literary manifestations; in the present work, these background factors become the chief objects of study. Dr. Jones is as much concerned with a revealing fact culled from an obscure newspaper or with the forgotten pages of fashion sheets and cook books as he is with the novels of Cooper or the poems of Bryant—perhaps even more so. He has pushed this point of view as far as it may be pushed—so far, indeed, that he may better be classed as a social than as a literary historian.

There are three aspects of American life, he believes, against which French cultural influences may be studied. These are the cosmopolitan spirit, which revealed itself in the theocratic colonies and the merchant classes of the seaboard; the frontier spirit, in the consideration of which he follows Turner's classic analysis; and finally the middle class spirit which developed from both groups—the product of the industrial revolution in America. If these three groups, says Dr. Jones, "are not the truth, they are something sufficiently near the truth for the pragmatic purposes of this study."

The second step in his introduction is a rapid survey of French immigration to the United States from the times of the explorers to those of 1815-1848, with their miscellaneous émigrés. In this section, as well as in the following, his dependence upon McMaster, Fäy, Chinard, and others is heavy. For primary sources he relies chiefly upon contemporary periodicals.

The body of the work itself suggests the barometer's chart more nearly than the architect's plan. French culture is analyzed through its manifestations rather than in terms of an arbitrary definition. It is followed with Boswellian patience and industry through the fields of American language, manners, art, religion (which merges into philosophy and on into educational theory and practice) and finally politics. Each of these topics receives chronological treatment, each is fully documented, and the conclusions of each are briefly summarized.

The final summary presents a "conclusion in which nothing is concluded." Perhaps it were better so, for Dr. Jones's thesis relates more to his method than to any definite conviction about the exact nature or extent of French influence.

> The situation is thus a dynamic rather than a static one. . . . To the frontier type of thinking, the French were simply another effete European nation to which the United States was obviously and providentially superior. To the cosmopolitan classes the regrettable crudities of American life seemed but the more crude beside the polish and superior *savoir faire* of the French. The middle classes vibrated between the two attitudes.

Dr. Jones's work is therefore exceedingly useful as a survey study of an influence which has, until now, received too little attention. It is particularly significant as a statement and an example of an extremist view of the function of the literary historian. It is interesting now because of the recent translation of Professor Fäy's similar work on the quarter century following the Declaration of Independence. But it must be followed by many more detailed and more thorough analyses of specific problems before general conclusions may be drawn with any degree of assurance.

7

1930

✤ TOWARDS STANDARDS: A STUDY OF ✤ THE PRINCIPAL CRITICAL MOVEMENT IN AMERICAN LETTERS
by Norman Foerster

By 1930 Norman Foerster had lost interest in the movement of which he was so important a part only a few years previously: the definition of a distinctively American literary tradition. He had instead joined forces with a small group of disciples of Irving Babbitt and Paul Elmer More to found the movement that came to be known as Neo-Humanism. As editor of the anthology *Humanism and America* in the same year, he became the center of a short-lived but intense critical controversy, but quickly faded in influence with the cause to which he so zealously committed his fortunes. When this review was written, enthusiasm was so high that it was not easy to see the fallacy in the argument and to attack the position of a leader to whom I owed so much of my own thinking up to that time. Both this and M. F. Brightfield's *The Issue in Literacy Criticism* (review 11, pp. 31-34) present the two principal antihistorical arguments then current in American literary criticism.

When Mr. Foerster's *American Criticism* appeared in 1928, the reviewers hastily turned the pages dealing with Poe, Lowell, Emer-

New York: Farrar and Rhinehart, 1930. Reviewed in Philadelphia *Public Ledger,* December 13, 1930.

son and Whitman, finally pouncing with all the enthusiasm they possessed upon the final chapter, a brief statement of the position of the "New Humanism" of twentieth century America. Some praised, some blamed; some signed on the dotted line, others bit their fingernails. But the issue had been cleared.

The present volume is little more than an amplification of that statement, a slight revision of which occupies its sixty climactic pages. In addition, we are given frontal attacks upon the critical attitudes of the impressionist and the sociological historian and chapters, first and last, relating the new movement to the Humanism (the capital letter is Mr. Foerster's) of the Renaissance and to the modern rather mild revival of purely religious enthusiasm.

Now that his creed is frankly and fully before us, we may ask to what extent his thought is original, to what extent it is clear, and of what importance it is both to the movement of which he is so wholly a part and to the contemporary spiritual welfare of the American mind. It would be futile to attempt here a statement or evaluation of "critical neo-humanism," the philosophical category in which Mr. Foerster classes his own mind.

The impression which this book leaves, in spite of its dogmatic precision of method, is not clear, and its author would be the last to claim originality independent of tradition. We are told that the Humanism of the Renaissance, like the humanism of today, was merely one statement of the belief in the duality of man and nature, and the assertion of the will and the wisdom of the human mind. But when we analyze the positive moral, ethical and aesthetic doctrines of, let us say, Erasmus, and compare them with those of, let us say, Irving Babbitt, we find little in common. And when we discover that Erasmus is charging at the windmills of scholasticism, whereas Mr. Babbitt is attacking those of deterministic science, we realize that the two movements, even in their negative aspects, have almost nothing in common. We conclude finally that the wisdom of the human mind is largely composed of minor follies; but here Mr. Foerster does not follow us, even though we are in the tradition of Erasmus. He takes the Emersonian path to the "exalted life" and trembles dangerously near the borderland of divine unity. If we are to live and thrive on human wisdom, we cannot so wholly banish irony from our counsels.

But this is almost a criticism of the movement rather than of Mr. Foerster, and thus we are brought to the real value of the book. Christianity had its Paul and Darwinism had its Huxley; every movement must have at least one fighting prophet to carry its vision into the strongholds of its various enemies. Neo-humanism has found Mr. Foerster, and in so far as the particular kind of humanism in which he so ardently believes is important, Mr. Foerster is important. That the movement is tonic to materialism-weary America must be admitted. That Mr. Foerster is an able and vigorous champion is beyond doubt.

8

1931

✈ AMERICAN HUMOR: A STUDY ✈
OF THE NATIONAL CHARACTER
by Constance Rourke

Constance Rourke was one of the most creative of the pioneers of the new American literary scholarship. Hers was the other side of Jones's study of the European background of our culture: the rooting of that culture in our native soil. The deceptively limited title of her first book, *American Humor,* kept many critics from appreciating the full importance of her discovery, and it was not until the folklorists and the anthropologists had provided the materials and a definition of national character that scholars like Henry Nash Smith, Daniel Hoffman, and R. W. B. Lewis had in hand a usable discipline for a fresh start on the problem of our national literature. Unhappily she did not live to complete the more definitive work that she planned, but her contribution in this book alone ensures her distinction. (See also review 16, pp. 48-51.)

The homespun native American makes his first bow in Miss Rourke's pages as the Yankee peddler, swapping his calicoes and his fabulous yarns with irresistible persuasion as he marches from the New England of his birth down a fertile Carolina valley or along the Ohio. In him humor and the epic spirit of the frontier are for the first time identified. He is followed closely by the backwoodsman with his exuberant confidence in himself, by the negro on the

New York: Harcourt, Brace and Company, 1931. Reviewed in *Saturday Review of Literature* 7 (April 18, 1931): 746-747.

Georgia plantation or the Mississippi River levee, and finally by the pioneers of the Crockett stamp and the gold seekers of '49. Talking, dancing, singing, and telling tall tales, these makers of the new America discovered folk bottoms of a native literature. The traditions of Europe and Africa were remembered, but only as seeds to be planted in a new soil and allowed to grow. America had been old because her cultures had been transplanted: when she became young at last, her youth was grotesque, prolonged, and ungoverned.

Miss Rourke thus probes her problem to its fundamentals and seeks an explanation for American humor in its folk epic element. A cursory examination of the origins of any other racial or national literature will quickly affirm the validity of her approach.

The second step in her study takes her inevitably to the stage, for it is in drama that the folk spirit of literate men first finds its ripe expression. Strolling players through the west and south used the cabin, the barn, and the river boat, and conspired with the minstrel, the burlesque, and the stock companies of the urban east to immortalize these native types. The Yankee in his gaudy Uncle Sam costume joins the backwoodsman and the negro in the specialty act and in the full-length comedy of manners. Even the American cockney is personified in Mike Fink, and innumerable others are added to the list. When at last this folk material found its way into journalism in the monologues of Artemus Ward and Josh Billings, its underlying philosophy was ready made and its forms and directions defined. Mark Twain and Bret Harte had some hankerings after a remembered and milder tradition, but the forces in themselves and in their environment were too strong for them.

Miss Rourke thus aligns herself with Lewis Mumford, Van Wyck Brooks, and those other literary historians who interpret broadly and sometimes superficially in terms of social movements and forces. But her penetration and grasp are sufficient to make her thought both illuminating and logical. So skillfully does she handle her material, that her conclusions, many of them sensational, seem almost too obvious for mention. This is especially true in her treatment of major American authors, many of them not ordinarily thought of as humorists at all. From humor in its superficial aspects she is carried down, willy-nilly, to the substrata of the American mind. The ratiocinations and the grotesque myth-making of Poe, the introspective lyricism of Emerson, the cosmic egoism of Thoreau and Whitman, all bow to their prototype, the Yankee Jack Dowling. In bald statement, such syntheses seem almost grotesque themselves, but in Miss Rourke's lucid mind, and even more lucid style, the march of their logic is irresistible. When we learn that Christopher Newman of *The American* (and oddly enough for a study of humor, Henry James receives almost twice as much attention as Mark Twain) is what he is because of this native tradition, we agree; and we understand better than we did why Robinson, Frost, and Sandburg are writing American literature, whereas Lowell, Longfellow, and Stedman for the most part were not.

The chief value of Miss Rourke's survey lies in her amazing power of critical synthesis. She introduces some new material and has depended almost entirely upon original sources. On the other hand, there are some rather obvious elements in American humor, such as the tales of Paul Bunyan and Tony Beaver, or the ballads of the cowboys and mountaineers, for which we might wish fuller treatment than is given them. But by restricting herself to the material which she considers of ultimate significance, by never departing for an instant from her thesis that humor is basically the expression of the folk epic spirit, and by maintaining her swift and lucid critical style at an even level, she has succeeded in writing, apparently almost by accident, the first satisfactory short history of native American literature.

9

1931

✿ THE REDISCOVERY OF THE FRONTIER ✿
by Percy H. Boynton

Percy Boynton, who taught American literature at the University of Chicago, was a scholar trained in the old school who nevertheless kept his mind open to the new currents. Picking up the theses of Parrington and Garland, he here makes a literal application of the Turner formula to literature. The contrast between the subtlety and depth of Constance Rourke's approach and the obvious force of Boynton's direct and simplistic method reflects credit on both—but who remembers Boynton's book today?

There has been need for many years of a treatment of the literary aspects of the American frontier commensurate, in incisive analysis of the problem, with Frederick J. Turner's classic essay, "The Significance of the Frontier in American History." The materials for such a study have been slowly accumulating, notably in R. L. Rusk's *The Literature of the Middle Western Frontier* and D. A. Dondore's *The Prairie and the Making of Middle America,* but neither L. L. Hazard's somewhat ecstatic *The Frontier in American Literature* nor Jay B. Hubbell's brief essay in "The Reinterpretation of Amercan Literature" fulfilled the need adequately. Mr. Boynton's small volume is the best generalization which has as yet appeared and should do much toward clarifying the lines of critical and historical approach to the problem.

Chicago: The University of Chicago Press, 1931. Reviewed in *Saturday Review of Literature* 8 (December 5, 1931): 343.

"The purpose of this study is more historical than critical," the author explains, but his attitude is not that of the scientifically objective historian. His primary object is the interpretation of literary history, an object which classes him with those critics who view literature as an organic part of social evolution and which makes him unavoidably a critic. He is extremely selective in the material which he treats, and he mentions no work without a brief appraisal of it in its relationship to his central thesis.

That thesis is derived directly from Turner. It is in brief that the frontier is the most significant single element in the development of the American nation, a movement which embraces in its larger aspects the problems of western expansion, of immigration, and even of those "back-trailers" who in successive waves have re-established the connections of new and primitive civilizations with the older homes of culture. Mr. Boynton's contributions lie in his grouping of the resultant literature under these three heads, in his distinctions between those writings which are literature and those which are merely source material for social history, and in his evaluations of the most important literary products of the movement.

A close correlation of literature with social history has its disadvantages as well as its advantages. Perhaps the most valuable chapter in this book is that on the "back-trailers," a term borrowed from Hamlin Garland and applied to all reactions to the frontier which took an Eastward direction. No other work has been so successful in establishing a basis for the study of the international novel and other aspects of the inevitable return of Americans to Europe. Henry James and William Dean Howells find here their logical places in American literary history as developments from the frustration of Mark Twain and the sentimentality of Bret Harte. The return to Europe is the climactic chapter in the story of the frontier.

On the other hand, Sinclair Lewis's *Dodsworth* by the same logic appears as a more profound and significant novel than *Main Street, Babbitt,* and *Arrowsmith,* a position which other critics may not be too willing to allow it. The consistent application of a thesis sometimes leads to strange conclusions in historical criticism, even though the positive values of such criticism may far overbalance the disadvantages of carrying an argument to its inevitable conclusion. Especially is this the case when the work in question is as entertaining and provocative—as logical and clear—as the one in review.

10

1931

CLASSIC AMERICANS: A STUDY OF EMINENT AMERICAN WRITERS FROM IRVING TO WHITMAN, WITH AN INTRODUCTORY SURVEY OF THE COLONIAL BACKGROUNDS OF OUR NATIONAL LITERATURE
by Henry Seidel Canby

Henry Canby was an editor and a teacher rather than primarily a literary critic, but his life as founding editor of the *Saturday Review of Literature* (successor to *The Literary Review* of the *New York Evening Post*) was dominated by a single idea. He was determined that the United States should have a new literary history based on the thesis that a literature is the expression of a people and that the American was a new man when he stepped off the ship onto this continent. Between his busy tasks in New York and New Haven, where he taught at Yale, he managed to write an introductory chapter on the colonial period, establishing his socioliterary approach, and some few chapters on major authors before giving up the project. *Classic Americans* was a stimulating book for me and was in part responsible for the friendship that led us to join forces in *Literary History of the United States* eight years later.

There is certain to be a surplus in the market for histories of American literature in the very near future. Two or more appeared last spring, and only a prophet who can survey at once the entire

---

New York: Harcourt Brace and Co., 1931. Reviewed in Philadelphia *Public Ledger*, October 3, 1931.

battlefield of the publishers could predict how many another two years will produce. That there will be many is certain.

The reason for the assurance behind this prediction is the great need for a good short history of the subject. Within the last five years our attitude toward it has completely changed. Instead of thinking of American as an offshoot of English literature, we now see that it is our principal means of understanding a civilization which has only just "come of age." This awakening has produced a multitude of books on major writers, literary tendencies and historical backgrounds. Someone must, sooner or later, condense all these findings and opinions into the pages of a simple short history of American literature.

Mr. Canby, as Yale professor of English and editor of a leading book review journal, has a position from which he could survey the problem as few others could. It is not surprising that he was tempted. Apparently he set to work some time ago at the beginning of his subject and collected material on Colonial and early national backgrounds, at the same time improving his very great knowledge of major American authors of the nineteenth century.

But the time was not ripe for the history toward which he was working. Wiser than some others, he decided to do well what could now be done—a book of appraisals of individuals against a background of the social and philosophical tendencies which have given shape to the literature of this country. The result is a well-proportioned volume of sane, clear, critical essays in the chronological order of their subjects.

In his estimates, Mr. Canby has kept in mind the recent findings and theories concerning his authors as well as the older scholarship and the writings of the authors themselves. He accepts and rejects this uneven mass of material with discrimination and judgment. We find that Irving "did little to illumine American life and character," that Cooper "for all his Quakerism and his Jeffersonian principles, was an aristocrat, and sometimes a snobbish aristocrat," that "Poe's virtuosity, true to the aims of journalism, is a technique for catching the attention of the reader," and that Whitman "was the first to give ordinary, vulgar, vital man a ranking with the captains and the kings." Such criticism has the spicy flavor of journalism at its best, supported by the sound knowledge which, unfortunately, journalism at its average does not seem to have.

11

1932

✒ THE ISSUE IN LITERARY CRITICISM ✒
by Myron F. Brightfield

By 1930 American literary history was well on the road toward a theory and a methodology of its own; but literary criticism had made no such progress. A work of literature could now be accounted for by something more than its "sources," but there was no firm authority—aesthetic, moral, or scientific—by which it could be evaluated apart from its historical context. As we have seen, Foerster in *Towards Standards* had attempted such a judicial base in a modern humanism that was both antihistorical and violently antiscientific; but the neohumanistic movement failed to take hold. Poe, Lowell, and Henry James, with their highly individual methods, were still left as the only American literary critics who even attempted a nonscientific standard of judgment and a consistent method of evaluation.

Meanwhile the objectivity and measurability of the new science offered various temptations. The two strongest were the Marxist dialectic and the Freudian psychopathology. V. F. Calverton and Granville Hicks (review 12, pp. 35-38) tried the first and Edmund Wilson, Ludwig Lewisohn, and others experimented with the second.

In *The Issue in Literary Criticism,* Myron Brightfield tried to simplify the problem by making literature itself, rather than literature as the expression of the social or psychological sciences, the material of the scientific method as developed in

Berkeley: University of California Press, 1932. Reviewed in *University of California Chronicle* 35 (January 1933): 152-154.

mathematics and physics. Reduced to its simplest terms: science
is art, art is science. His argument may not seem valid today
but it is important for what it reveals of its time. Both literary
history and literary criticism were to remain faithful to their
realities in aesthetics and to use science only as an anchor
in time and space. By 1930, literary history was moving beyond
political and economic determinism, and literary criticism
was moving away from both historical and judicial criteria
into a "pure" aestheticism founded on contextual analysis.
With Ransom, Tate, Cleanth Brooks, and many others, the
New Criticism became the dominant school for the next twenty
years.

Ever since the days of Taine, the effort to apply the methods of
science to literary criticism has been continuous, but, for the most
part, unavailing. This tendency has become much accentuated in
recent years by the vigorous movement among social historians
toward scientific thought and the discrediting of Clio, a muse. As
alchemy became chemistry, as astrology became astronomy, and as
the medicine man, with his humors and his herbs, became the bac-
teriologist, so the "literary" historian is giving way to the scientific
historian, and the political economist (with whom Carlyle did such
valiant battle) has disappeared to make place for the economist, the
sociologist, and the political scientist. In the beginning was the
λόγος, [word], but in the present is the μετρικός, [measure]. Religion
and art have alone succeeded in maintaining the old method, and in
both of them it has been seriously challenged.

Mr. Brightfield's thesis makes a frontal attack upon the traditional methods in literary criticism. It differs, however, from most
such attacks in that it divorces literature completely from the social
and natural sciences, defines an autonomous province for all art,
and attempts to provide an empirical method within that province.
It thus avoids altogether the pitfalls of materialism and mechanism,
and of confusion with the problems of history, the social and natural
sciences, and psychology. The issue in literary criticism, as he sees
it, is that between idealistic and pragmatic systems of metaphysics,
and between the deductive and the inductive methods of logic; and
not that between the humanist and his opponents of various kinds,
except in so far as such views may be reduced to philosophical terms.

His position is so clearly stated and so logically developed that it readily lends itself to summary: The controversy among the impressionists, the naturalists, the mechanists, the vitalists, the neo-humanists, and the modified humanists is beside the point. The method of science premises "knowledge based upon a standard as impersonal and as free from private whim or prejudice as is humanly possible— for only such knowledge can be verified adequately by another." The scientific method proceeds by three stages: hypothesis; empirical examination of data "which can be observed, measured, and tested"; and a check of findings against other such investigations independently conducted, and against experience. Philosophy has provided two irreconcilable systems of thought: the idealistic, which proceeds from unverifiable (except by intuition) premises, by deductive reasoning, to humanly satisfying conclusions; and the empirical, which proceeds from hypotheses based upon observable and measurable data, by inductive reasoning, to conclusions which may be tested by human experience. The deductive method of the idealist has been discredited in the fields of the natural sciences; it is presumably in the process of being discredited in the fields of the social sciences; in the fields of literature and art it has so far succeeded in maintaining its authority, but its validity is subject to question. An aesthetic may be formulated in empirical terms by defining the beautiful as "a term applied by a man to an object (or situation) to indicate that the object (or situation) is in a state in which he wishes it to be." As this state is usually that of a possibility or probability rather than that of an actuality, the artist devotes himself to the statement of attainable desire rather than of attained actuality. All art is therefore fiction, but the highest art (one might almost say the only true art, although Mr. Brightfield does not carry his argument quite to this point) is the statement of a desire for a probability, because improbable possibility is in a degree false, and impossibility is completely false except in so far as it excites in the artist or reader, or both, desire *toward* a possible standard of conduct. "The activities of the critic are thus directed to the task of determining, on the basis of the materials at his disposal, whether the author's pattern can be successfully applied to the final end or aim which has controlled its construction."

A fundamental disagreement with Mr. Brightfield's position and a defense of idealism is both possible and tempting, but it would not be profitable in so limited a space. Even a systematic analysis of his book for the purpose of discovering flaws in his logic, with his premises accepted for the purposes of argument, must be foregone for the same reasons. I shall content myself with the statement of a few of the more obvious advantages and difficulties of his position as they occur to me:

Advantages: (1) By eliminating cant and vague terminology and by adopting the idiom of philosophy alone, he has reduced the current debate to simple terms and cleared the issues. (2) By distinguishing scientific (inductive, empirical) *method* as a thought process applicable to literary criticism from the materials and specific applications of natural and other sciences, he has established literary and art criticism in a field of their own, and he has answered any arrogant claims for its jurisdiction by workers in other fields. (3) By linking literary criticism with literary history ("Literary history *is* literary criticism") as aspects of the same integral process, subject to the same laws and working by the same methods, he has exonerated the empirical critic or historian from the accusation of pedantry.

Difficulties: (1) By his use of the terms "poetic truth" and "empirical idealism" he has opened himself to the charge of ambiguity, or even to that of resorting, in the final analysis, to some of the mystical and intuitive machinery of his opponents. (2) By making its effect upon conduct the final test of excellence in literature or art, he has limited his aesthetic to moral judgment and eliminated the element of pleasure, except as a derivative of good, as a criterion. (3) By striving for almost complete objectivity in dealing with the data of the human imagination, he has encountered far greater obstacles than those encountered in dealing with the data of non-human nature. These obstacles, which have proved to be, in some minds, insuperable in the social sciences, are even greater in the fields of literature and art. (4) By setting up the standard of fictional probability as the measure of art, he has ranked the realistic novel or drama as the highest and lyric poetry as the lowest of literary media. This reversal of traditional values, to which he is inevitably led by the logic of his argument, seems to me to constitute the most serious difficulty of all in his position, and to make its acceptance virtually impossible.

12

1933

✣ THE GREAT TRADITION ✣
by Granville Hicks

I had the honor of twice introducing Granville Hicks to scholarly audiences—once in the 1930s when, as editor of *The New Masses,* he was wholly committed to the Marxist party line, and again some years later when he had wholly renounced it in his novel *Only One Storm* (1942). Even though it covers only the latter half of American literature, *The Great Tradition* was the most successful effort to apply this thesis to American literary history, its only serious rival being V. L. Calverton's *The Liberation of American Literature* (1932). Although I personally rejected the close tie with the Communist party and philosophy, I must admit to having been, with Parrington and many others at this time, deeply influenced by the political and economic determinism of the Marxian school. Hicks later joined forces with us in the Canby tradition and contributed a regular column to the *Saturday Review.*

Mr. Hicks has caused something more than a ripple in the waters of American criticism by this history of our literature. It covers, more or less chronologically, the period from the Civil War to the present day, with a brief preliminary chapter on the "heritage" of the New England Group. But its distinguishing feature is the theory of literary criticism which underlies its narrative. Mr. Hicks believes that literature is determined by the social forces which shape the

New York: The Macmillan Co., 1933. Reviewed in *American Literature* 6 (November 1934): 358-361.

environment in which it appears, and that the central social force in American civilization is the slow coming of Marxian Communism.

The first of these beliefs is now no novelty to students of American literary history. When V. L. Parrington, in 1927, boldly reviewed the history of American thought in terms of Jeffersonian agrarianism, the elder critics received their first major shock; but the way was once and for all time opened to a reinterpretation of our literary history. The language link with English literature, which had previously made it impossible to consider American writings in terms of the forces which conditioned their production, no longer could bind so tightly. The protest against "mental slavery," which was voiced by Cooper, Channing, and Emerson a century before, had found adequate grounds. Subsequent research and criticism in American literature have proceeded on the axiom that a mature civilization should look to its literary past for the factors which determined its mental growth.

Mr. Hicks is an extremist in his acceptance of this view. His individual literary judgments, as well as his general principles of historical interpretation, are largely determined by it. He does not make the mistake of believing that a writer is an artist merely because he gives expression to native and contemporary realities, but his aesthetic judgments are so far colored by his deterministic views as to fail frequently of objectivity. A few examples will illustrate the point. After recognizing the "flawless metaphor" of *Moby Dick,* he stresses the comparative failure of this "metaphysical epic" to grasp "all the principal varieties of experience" in its era. The timeless theme of obsession in Ahab, suggestive of Aeschylus, Shakespeare, and Dostoevsky, is subordinated by this critic to the demand that Melville interpret the whole thought of a particular time and place. Whitman is more fortunate in his hands, because his cosmic intuition was in harmony with his understanding of America, the common man, and the meaning of the frontier; and we are not surprised at rediscovering the weaknesses of Lowell, Aldrich, and Stedman. The positive values of Howells as recorder of the contemporary scene are brought out with a deserved emphasis, but he is judged to be weak because he was "wrong on many [social] issues" rather than because a conventional ethic hampered his understanding of essential human nature and because he could not free himself from the formal limitations of the popular romance of his day. The judgment of Emily Dickinson suggests Macaulay's classic misinterpretation of Boswell: that his strength lay in his weakness. Negative virtues, thinks Mr. Hicks, made her "tower over other poets of the period," but "she could have none of the vigor that is found in an artist for whom self-expression is also the expression of the society of which he is a part." Norris and Sinclair failed, he says, only because they did not fully assimilate their material, but they were on the right track.

Mr. Hicks lays too much emphasis in all his judgments on the writer's ability to understand and express the society in which he lives; too little on his comprehension of more nearly absolute values and recurrent qualities in nature and human nature. And he pays too little attention to a writer's style and mastery of his art. The work of authors like Hawthorne, Melville, Dickinson, James, Henry Adams, E. A. Robinson, and Robert Frost fail, in his hands, of adequate and discriminating appreciation because the sources of their inspiration and the qualities of their art are too subjective, and because they express a social philosophy which is opposed to his. By demanding always the epic in preference to the lyric or other forms of the imagination, the social rather than the individual comprehension, Mr. Hicks has closed his mind to a good half of human experience. On the other hand, authors like Howells, Crane, Norris, and notably John Dos Passos, gain through an emphasis upon one or more of their principal virtues. His derogatory criticism, in these cases, is more acceptable because he is asking for the thing which these writers were attempting to supply; but even here the highly specialized basis of his thought makes him fail in well-rounded judgment.

I hesitate to quarrel with Mr. Hicks on the dogma that Marxian Communism is the ultimate formula of American society and that our writings up to this time which point toward its consummation are in "the great tradition." I am not convinced that this is true; neither am I sure that it is false. A conviction on this point would have to be, as it is in Mr. Hicks, a matter of faith. The evidence is, up to this time, insufficient to prove it. It is a fact that social protest, particularly in the decades between 1890 and 1910, furnished a predominating theme in our literature, and it is also true that our literature today is socially conscious in a broader and more fundamental way than it ever has been. This does not, however, lead me to turn away from the critical method of objective analysis of all the causal factors of literary production and from the intuitive appreciation of beauty and truth where I find it. I am no more willing to accept Mr. Hicks's formula as final than I am to be content with that of Parrington, the similar Marxian formula of Calverton, or the Freudian-Puritan formula of Lewisohn. All of these challengers are stimulating, but they are ultimately valuable only when the arbitrary barriers in their thought are broken down; when their findings are related, the one to the other; and when the whole problem is reexamined in terms of a broader understanding of the human experience than any one of them will allow.

It may seem paradoxical to conclude by saying that Mr. Hicks's book seems to me to be one of the best rapid surveys of the later American literature that I have read. He has rather more aesthetic sensibility than other social interpreters of our literature have demonstrated, and the restricted and dogmatic formula of his thought has afforded him the means for a swift and clear charting of his course through a mass of reading which has left many critics in mental confusion. Furthermore, he seems to have read carefully the works upon which he comments, and he has depended consistently upon his own reactions rather than on the repeated words of censure and praise of earlier critics. His book is one to be referred to and reckoned with by any student who ventures into his field, but it has the virtues and the defects of an original piece of historical criticism rather than those which make for ultimate acceptance as authority. We need more literary histories as conscientious, consistent, and adventurous as this.

13

1951 [1934]

EXILE'S RETURN: A LITERARY ODYSSEY OF THE NINETEEN-TWENTIES
Revised and Expanded with a New Foreword and Concluding Chapter
by Malcolm Cowley

Malcolm Cowley once wrote to me that a publisher had asked him to do a short history of American literature and that he would like to discuss with me the nineteenth-century story because he knew it only as background for what he knew otherwise so well, the literary experience of the American in the first half of the twentieth century. As far as I know, his history was never written, but his own part of it is in this book. Anyone who does not absorb and understand *Exile's Return* is not prepared to comment on any American literary event between 1915 and 1975. This is a comparatively minor revision of the *Exile's Return* of 1934, which contributed so much toward an understanding of the theme of alienation in the writers of the interbellum period.

This is the inside story of the literary generation of the twenties. Written as a sort of confessional, it has become, in the two decades since it first appeared, a classic document in literary history. Inspired obviously by the author's need to understand himself, it is the autobiography of a literary movement. No one has done the job better than Malcolm Cowley, although many have tried.

New York: The Viking Press, 1951. Reviewed in *American Quarterly* 3 (Fall 1951): 273-275.

Mr. Cowley's thesis is simple. To have been born between 1892 and 1900 was to have reached maturity just as the world turned upside down. But the experience of the First World War by America's then young men was not merely a disillusionment, as most critics have assumed. This was a special severance from the past, a cutting of roots, symbolized by the Norton-Harjes Ambulance Corps. These college boys were not soldiers, they were spectators of a great adventure. They were helping to fight someone else's war, and either way they could not lose. They might be killed of course, but that would only make the danger valid. "We were seeing a great show. . . . Danger made it possible once more to write about love, adventure, death." (pp. 40, 42).

The experience of exile is the key to the attitude which turned this generation into the first major American literary group since Emerson, Poe, Hawthorne, and Melville. "Aesthetic standards of judgment, after being applied to works of art, had been applied to the careers of their authors and finally to the world at large." (p. 103) "The religion of art . . . furnished them with ideals of workmanship that gave them a steady purpose in the midst of their dissipations." (p. 286) Here are Fitzgerald, Hemingway, Dos Passos, Faulkner; here are Pound, Eliot, Cummings, Hart Crane. These young men sailed from the "French Line Pier" (symbol of voluntary exile after the war) for a Paris that never was, a Parnassus from whose heights the world could be viewed. Dada supplied the meaningless ritual of their new religion of art in its first phase of protest, but Dada had a history in French art and the Americans followed clues back to earlier and more meaningful phases of the movement. They found Mallarmé and Valéry while they played around with Aragon. Then Dada died and they came home.

Cowley's third major symbol is the suicide of Harry Crosby. In this revision he admits that it was Hart Crane that he wanted to write about, that he had to understand, but Crane was too close. He could make the point by telling Crosby's story, the life of the exile who did not return—or rather, returned only to die a few years sooner than he had planned and so bring a literary decade to a close. While the new writers were abroad, the older ones, with the aid of history, had made American literature important. In December 1930, the Swedish Academy awarded the Nobel Prize to its first

American, Sinclair Lewis. Lewis was not one of the exiles—he was older—but he tried to explain them. A masterpiece of good will, the speech of acceptance of this acid man confused the aims of the two literary generations, so near to each other in years, so far apart in experience. The new group did not wish to give America "a literature worthy of her vastness." They merely wished "to protray the lives and hearts of individual Americans" and so "suggest the larger picture." They had a new "ideal of perfection gained from their study of foreign writers and they wanted to apply the ideal at home." (p. 298)

Malcolm Cowley is their chronicler because he did not commit suicide; he bought a farm in Connecticut. He was the Ishmael of his generation. "Why then does anyone step forth?" There was one who was detached even from aesthetic detachment and he was to tell the tale. Perhaps his literary creed, which differed slightly from that of his friends but had much in common with the earlier Mencken and the later Wolfe, made it possible for him to advise Hart Crane— not quite in time—and to write, "I believed that the man of letters, while retaining his own point of view, which was primarily that of a poet, should concern himself with every department of human activity, including science, sociology, and revolution." (p. 160) His social consciousness and his selflessness made him the critic and chronicler of his generation. At every turn of his narrative he could write in 1934 and repeat in 1951, "As I said at the time." His steady, warm, slightly amused and critical eye is still triangulating his generation. Only a brief prologue, an epilogue, and a few paragraphs to make explicit some of the subtleties that had only been inferred were necessary to bring up to date this appraisal and explanation of the "lost generation." No one is likely to do the job better.

14

1937

THE FLOWERING OF NEW ENGLAND by Van Wyck Brooks

With this book, American literary history came into its own with Book-of-the-Month Club adoption and best-seller status. I was not alert enough to appreciate it immediately but later wrote this review for the journal of the Historical Society of Pennsylvania. After that, I reviewed each of the five volumes of what Brooks later called the "Makers and Finders" series as it appeared.

In *America's Coming of Age* (1915) and other early works, Brooks rejected the "genteel tradition" in American letters and urged the discovery of an indigenous culture that would provide a "usable past" for a new literature. In attempting to solve his own psychocultural dilemma, he himself had a breakdown. When he returned a few years later to a normal life of writing, his "usable past" had become a simple chronicle of what the literary life in itself had meant and could mean in America. Starting with the New England renaissance, he attempted a composite picture of the American writer by reading all the letters, journals, and autobiographical works of all the writers, great and minor, of a particular cultural crisis. The result was a series of volumes that ran together in something of a chronological sequence but that were actually separate studies of different periods and cultural centers. His method was to accumulate myriads of little slips containing

New York: E. P. Dutton and Co., Inc., 1937. Reviewed in *Pennsylvania Magazine of History and Biography* 62 (January 1938): 109-111.

quotations and then to weave them together into a connected narrative. No one has ever succeeded in imitating his special charm and his vivid portraits of a people. It is not literary history, it is not cultural history, it is the work of a genre painter in words.

The only justification for reviewing a popular book a year or more after its appearance is a conviction that it contains some of the elements of a classic. In these terms further comment on the most widely and favorably reviewed non-fiction work of the past year is more than warranted. *The Flowering of New England* should not, and probably will not, pass into the limbo.

The enduring quality of this study of the literary and cultural history of New England in the nineteenth century depends upon its success in bringing to life rather than in merely analyzing a phase of our intellectual development; upon its significance as the culmination of the thought of perhaps the foremost of our living literary critics; and upon its own readability and literary excellence.

Mr. Brooks has attained that view of his subject which is rare among literary historians: the realization that the whole is greater than any of its parts. Although his method is roughly chronological and he devotes separate chapters to individual writers, he never loses sight for a moment of the fact that his subject is the New England mind of the nineteenth century, and that that mind is a complete organism with a life cycle of its own. It is hard enough to write a biography of a man or woman; it requires genius to write a biography of a people. Gibbon succeeded in doing so; Carlyle to a lesser degree. *The Flowering of New England* is of the genre of *The Decline and Fall* and *The French Revolution.* Starting with the portraits of Gilbert Stuart and concluding with Emerson's spiritual grasp of the meaning of his times, Mr. Brooks has produced a single work of art, not a chronicle. The book is a whole of which every part—the histories of Prescott, Brook Farm, Thoreau at Walden, Longfellow at Cambridge—reveals its meanings only with reference to a central and all-pervading significance.

The thematic structure of *The Flowering of New England* originates in and returns to Emerson, for it was the Concord sage who taught Mr. Brooks what life is all about. His early blasts against

Puritanism were, like those of H. L. Mencken, mere evidences of
that hopeless but provocative revolt against Puritan values which
started with Roger Williams, and shaped the lives of Edwards,
Channing, Hawthorne, and Emerson himself. Each revolutionist
has in the end only reasserted the faith of his fathers that human
life is best understood in terms of moral values: his revolt has been
successful to the extent that he has justified his right to rediscover
moral values for himself instead of accepting the findings and formu-
lations of the fathers. Mr. Brooks's intellectual history seems to
have followed somewhat the same pattern. It has been concerned
with the problem of the artist in a materialistic civilization. Given
an America of apparently infinite natural resources, a laissez faire
economy, a deterministic and materialistic metaphysics, and a pragmatic morality could have been foretold from the start [sic]. The
function of literature in such an intellectual atmosphere is obviously
that of recording phenomena, not of evaluating principles. Realism
was predicted in the work of Cooper and Irving, in spite of the valiant
efforts of Poe to correct this tendency and to formulate an aesthetic.
With the opening of the West, the problem again became acute, even
more so than in the early phases of our intellectual history. Mark
Twain attempted to face the problem and was defeated; Henry
James recognized the problem and ran away from it. What did
Emerson do about it? Did he recognize it? Did he accept it? Did he
run away from it? Apparently he found a way.

   The Ordeal of Mark Twain and *The Pilgrimage of Henry James*
are among the most profound and challenging of our critical studies
of our own literature. Both are perversely wrong in their conclusions, both issue challenges which subsequent critics cannot ignore.
Whatever conclusions he may reach about the meaning of the work
of these two men, each critic must now start with the problem as
Mr. Brooks states it. How can the literary artist in America remain
faithful to the material he knows from experience and extract from
that material a central aesthetic significance? He states the case
himelf in his *Sketches in Criticism:* "Before the emergence of our
critical movement, the clear sense of the great values of life had long
been submerged in America. . . . Our thought has been centrifugal
instead of centripetal; it has gone out to the frame, it has never
fixed itself upon the picture." Mr. Brooks fixed his thought finally

upon a picture which turned out to be a portrait of Emerson.

The story behind the writing of his life of Emerson would be interesting if we could know it in detail. Obviously it is the record of a spiritual struggle. The book appeared in two forms, and was imperfect at the end. First came *Emerson and Others,* with six chapters on episodes in the life of the essayist: then an interval of some years; and finally, the completed narrative. The lives of Mark Twain and of Henry James had been studies in defeat, and much of that of Emerson was written in a tone of almost patronizing pity. But in his final sentence the biographer granted to his subject "the universe in which to live." There is in these words something of the effect of the sun finally breaking through storm clouds on the evening of a threatening day. Had Mr. Brooks solved his problem for himself?

The Flowering of New England provides evidence for an affirmative answer to that question. The individual artist has become reconciled to his environment because he has found a way to retain his integrity and at the same time allow the environment to be the hero of the story. This is the only possible answer to materialistic determinism and the challenge of nineteenth-century science. Emerson—and Mr. Brooks—are supreme because they have subordinated their egotism to the life forces which work upon them, and have found, to their surprise, that those forces are friendly. In these terms, the artist may once again function.

It were superfluous to repeat again the comments upon the literary values of the resulting book. Mr. Brooks is very free with his sources, weaving them into a pattern rather than piecing them together by a deliberate historical process. The result is subject to the criticisms of misrepresentation and error of detail. But these weaknesses are more than compensated by centrality of understanding and living quality in the narrative. In such work only is the literary historian both artist and critic. Only a genius should attempt it; but Mr. Brooks has succeeded at last.

15

1931

STUDIES IN LITERARY TYPES IN SEVENTEENTH-CENTURY AMERICA, 1607-1710, IN TWO PARTS
by Josephine K. Piercy

In the old days before the New Criticism and Structuralism, literature was usually taught by "appreciation," "philology" (or the history of language), and "literary types" (novel, drama, poetry, essay). Most American literature of the colonial period was too documentary for any of these approaches and so was often left to the historians or altogether ignored. Most of it fell into such categories as the polemical tract, the sermon, or the history of God's providence and therefore did not lend itself to literary study. Josephine Piercy was a pioneer in that she attempted in this book to adapt the "literary types" approach to non-belles lettres. Not an intrinsically profound book, this definition of literary types in American literature of the seventeenth century helped to make these earliest years a part of the whole history of American literature.

The problem with which this thesis deals is of the greatest importance to the historian of American literature. If that history be limited to belles lettres, there is little before 1790 that is worthy of discussion. On the other hand, a definition which ignores form in the interest of content, allows no exclusion of the written word. Some inclusive yet limited test for the recognition of literature in the Colonial period is badly needed.

Yale Studies in English, vol. 91. New Haven: Yale University Press, 1939. Reviewed in *Journal of English and Germanic Philology* 40 (July 1941): 424.

Miss Piercy assumes that consciousness of type is sufficient. She rests her case on whether or not there is, in the first century of our literary history, "sufficient repetition of kind to indicate awareness of literary composition." This awareness usually includes an implied or explicit theory of style and form. In the writings of Cotton Mather she finds all of these elements in abundance, and she uses him as the measure of his antecedents. Quoting Captain John Smith, she asserts that many writings of the early period which can by these tests be clearly defined as literature, "haue been diuersly traduced by variable judgements of Times opinionists." She answers these "opinionists" by defining and discussing about a half dozen "literary" types.

As her findings are more suggestive than conclusive, she is wise in calling her monograph "studies," a word which commits her to no final judgment of the issue. Her study is not sufficiently exhaustive, especially in writings of colonies other than New England and in types other than the theological. In certain cases in which she does venture afield, as in that of the scientific essay, she confuses content with form and wanders from her path. Although she has several chapters on English and classical influences, the relative degrees of originality and imitation in any specific case are never quite clear. As an "essay," in Montaigne's sense, her thesis is suggestive, but the "Times opinionists" are not yet fully answered.

16

1940

THE COURSE OF AMERICAN DEMOCRATIC THOUGHT
by Ralph H. Gabriel

While the revolution in the discipline of literary history—particularly American literary history—was moving forward, American historians themselves were going through a parallel upheaval. When Turner's classic address, "The Significance of the Frontier in American History" (1893), appeared as the title essay in his book on the frontier in 1920, its full impact had already been felt, and many American historians had turned from the old military, constitutional, and political disciplines to a concept of history based on all aspects of a developing culture. Not only did they include other forces and currents borrowed from the emerging social and behavioral sciences, but they were writing histories of religion, art, literature, and ideas in themselves. By 1940, the profession was ready for a restudy of the American past in two books based squarely on the new discipline of intellectual history: Ralph Gabriel's *The Course of American Democratic Thought* (1940) and Merle Curti's *The Growth of American Thought* (1943). Rebellious literary historians like Parrington, Foerster, and Matthiessen had already turned away from the old bondage to English philology and had created forms of intellectual history based on a new reading of American literature as the expression of the developing American culture.

New York: The Ronald Press Company, 1940. Reviewed in *American Literature* 12 (November 1940): 362-363.

Now the time had come for the two movements to merge into one, forming, first, departments in the universities and then, in the early 1950s, a national society of American Studies in which Ralph Gabriel, Charles Barker, George Taylor, and other intellectual historians could rub shoulders with Carl Bode, Kenneth Murdock, and others on the literary side, including myself. We were facing the same historical problems in parallel and mutually helpful ways. Ralph Gabriel's book was a major influence in moving my thought from the politico-economic determinism of Parrington to a broader view of the relationships between literature and the history of ideas as determining factors in the growth of American civilization.

It was inevitable that someone should attempt to apply the Love-joy technique of intellectual history to the development of American democratic theory. Mr. Gabriel, in so doing, has produced a stimulating and provocative study of nineteenth-century America, with the faults and blessings of that technique upon its head.

The first task of such an historian is to select two or three dominant ideas which have exhibited themselves during a given period of time and among a specific people or peoples, but in a wide variety of contexts and with many incidental variations in their manifestations. The ideas here selected are individualism, moral law, and progress. Of these three is the theory of American democracy composed in its pure form.

The second task of our historian is to select the pre-eminent exponents of these ideas from various fields of thought. In this instance Emerson, Thoreau, Melville, and Whitman represent the men of letters: Royce and William James the philosophers; F. J. Turner and Henry Adams the historians; Lincoln, Calhoun, Theodore Roosevelt, and Wilson the politicians; Gladden, Bliss, Sheldon, and Rauschenbusch the men of religion; Field and Holmes the jurists; Carnegie the man of wealth; Ward, Morgan, and Sumner the natural scientists; Henry George, Bellamy, Veblen, Ely, and the Saratoga revolters the social scientists; and a number of others. The array of names is imposing.

The third task is to distinguish a limited number of definable manifestations of the ideas of individualism, moral law, and progress as illustrated and promoted by these men and their lesser followers. This is accomplished by studies of the "pre-Sumter" period, the period of the War, the Gilded Age, the Age of Progress, and the immediate past. Thus are passed in review the movements of nationalism, the Gospel of Wealth, economic and scientific determinism, philosophical neorationalism and idealism, the religion of humanity, the Progressive movement in politics, and the humanistic and positivist movement in contemporary economics.

The result of this classification and analysis of ideas as currents is a single, more or less clearly defined, theory. Mr. Gabriel sees the central doctrines of American democracy as by-products of the eighteenth-century enlightenment, dividing at the time of the Civil War into two main currents: that which led into what he calls "humanism," and that which followed the stream of materialistic determinism to its logical and defeatist results. His sympathy is with the former trend and he sees in conclusion a survival of the faith because of its very adaptability to complex and conflicting influences. "The democratic faith is, then, in essence, a philosophy of the mean. It proclaims that, within broad limits of an ordered nature, man is master of his destiny." Thus he implied that the modern American democrat may still fight against extremists and fanatics in church, state, society, his own soul, and other nations as he has persistently fought for a century and a half. The cause is not yet lost. The historian himself stops short of raising the banner over the armies of the present, but he brings it up to the firing line.

The timeliness of such a study is obvious, and its fundamental soundness is not easy to question. Even the casual student of America's recent past could reach a similar conclusion on far less evidence. Nor would an exhaustive analysis of every thinker and every trend of thought in the American mind bring a result very different. The value of the book is that it produces sufficient evidence to establish a position without belaboring or overloading the main issue.

The weakness of the method is that its selection of materials is highly eclectic and its organization of them largely arbitrary. Many men and movements of equal importance with those discussed are merely referred to in passing or are ignored. Chronological sequence gives way in the interest of following through developments in a given field of thought and of conforming to the pattern of the text. Finally, there is some confusion between the view of the historical critic in retrospect and that of the mass mind at the time that events took place and thoughts were expressed. The historical critic evaluates Melville's skepticism highly, but his contemporaries almost wholly ignored it. The present-day economist does not attach the same importance to the Single Tax program of Henry George as did his almost fanatical followers. Mr. Gabriel is sometimes in the past with the men and movements he is discussing, sometimes in the present expressing his own and the contemporary view of past events.

But to say these things is not to assign his book to the discard. For some years we have had a sufficiency of literal and objective historical research and writing. The appearance of an appraisal of American democratic thought in historical perspective is welcome, even though the technique employed is insufficiently developed as yet to make such work definitive as well as provocative.

17

1941

AMERICAN RENAISSANCE: ART AND EXPRESSION IN THE AGE OF EMERSON AND WHITMAN
by F. O. Matthiessen

Matthiessen was always something of a maverick in the profession. One of the pioneering founders of the famous Salzburg seminar after World War II, he was neither a member of the Modern Language Association nor was he in *Who's Who;* yet he was a member of the team that initiated the degree of the History of American Civilization at Harvard and, until his suicide in 1950, was perhaps the most original and dynamic leader of the movement for the restudy of American literary history. In the late 1930s he and I were giving parallel seminars on the major romantic writers—Emerson, Thoreau, Melville, and Whitman—and we had many direct and indirect exchanges.

What we were both trying to discover was a way to maintain the Parrington approach to literary history on the *horizontal,* time-line plane and yet to place and explain the master artist and the master work that rose above and sank below such conditioning factors and produced the "great" works of the "great" artists. Matty broke the barrier by using the psychological and aesthetic instruments to establish a *vertical* approach to the problem. In this he was aided by his teacher John Livingston Lowes, whose *Road to Xanadu* reflected the current knowledge of depth psychology (Freud, Jung, and others), and by his study of T. S. Eliot, whose theory that "the existing monuments [of art] form an ideal order" had been expounded in the essay "Tradition and Individual Talent." The result was *American Renaissance,* which gave the vertical dimension to the new literary history as Parrington had provided the horizontal.

At this point I quote two letters that Matty wrote to me about this time: the first after I had reviewed his book in the *Saturday Review of Literature* and the second when I, as chairman of the American Literature Group of the Modern Language Association, had invited him to participate in the program of the annual meeting.

Old Ferry Lane
Kittery, Maine
June 26, [1941]

Dear Spiller,

I want to thank you for your criticism in the *Saturday Review.* You could hardly have evaluated my book in terms that could have gratified me more. I was delighted that you singled out the democratic strain, which no other reviewer so far has given the weight which seems to me to attach to it. In fact you are the one reviewer who has spoken out of the depth of knowledge of the subject that makes me respect the verdict—and hence be especially warmed by it.

I was interested in what you said about *The Road to Xanadu* since I had not had Mr. Lowes consciously in mind at any time while writing this book. His concern with Coleridge was so much in the psychology of creation rather than in the created work that I felt that I was following much more the leads given me by Emerson and the Transcendentalists themselves. But as you may know, I wrote my thesis under Lowes, and have admired him greatly, so here is probably one of my central debts, so close that I didn't see it.

I wish that our paths crossed more often, since I'd like to catch up on your own major lines of current interest.

Cordially yours,
F. O. Matthiessen

Old Ferry Lane
Kittery, Maine
September 15, [1941]

Dear Spiller,

I was very glad to have your letter. I am afraid that I must appear to many as hopelessly intransigent and perfectionist in my attitude toward the M.L.A., but the standards engendered by its existence have long seemed to me productive of more harm than good. And I have felt no vital function performed by the annual meetings where far too many unrelated papers are read with no opportunity for adequate discussion. Your projected group for this year sounds potentially far more fruitful, and if I hadn't already made some engagements for that week in New York, I might be tempted to try again. At any rate I am deeply grateful for your generous invitation to participate.

It's not that I'm negligent of the possibilities of group action. For instance I've been willing to sit through five day sessions of the national convention of the Teachers Union, since beyond the boredom of the protracted parliamentary proceedings there emerged real struggles and issues, real controversy and discussion on major questions for educators and I could come away with the sense I had become a more integral part of an important social movement. But from my contacts with the M.L.A. I have had the sense that most of the papers were delivered for pure professionalism, i.e., either to gain jobs or to show off. At least no atmosphere was created that challenged my thought either as a teacher or a writer.

Well, you hardly asked for all this, and must forgive my thinking out loud this way. Thanks again for your friendly interest, and I'm looking forward to your review of my book in *American Literature*.

Cordially yours,
F. O. Matthiessen

Matty was too complicated a genius to survive, as so often happens. These are the people from whom we learn the basic and eternal truths, but his final days were complicated by deep personal problems and by his emotional interest in the Russian takeover of Czechoslovakia. Yet in this book he gave the American Romantic movement its own roots in European social theory and philosophy, bypassing the British except as an influence among others, and so tied our thinking to Herder, Hegel, Freud, and Jung and to the nonhistorical traditions of masterworks of art. The first review was for the general reader; the review in *American Literature* was designed to speak to a professional audience.

REVIEW 1

The appearance of another critical estimate of the literary great of our past century will be greeted with enthusiasm or alarm or weariness depending upon the mood of the reader. There is no shortage of such works. Separate biographies and criticisms of Emerson, Thoreau, Melville, Hawthorne, and Whitman line our library shelves; and syntheses of the facts and theories which surround their works have been many, from Mumford's *The Golden Day* to Brooks's *The Flowering of New England.* The reasons for another such study, especially for one of more than six hundred pages, must be convincing.

The chief reasons are two, a need and its answer, and together they are extremely convincing. In an era of crisis, a people naturally turns to its historians and critics and prophets for reassurance of its faith in its own destiny. Mr. Matthiessen combines some of the characteristics of all three types of leader. He knows and has meditated long and profoundly on the literary history of America and its antecedents in Western European culture; he has developed his own technique of literary criticism under the best of contemporary masters, Brooks, Eliot, Lowes, and many others; and because he is ultimately concerned with values rather than with mere facts, the robe of the prophet falls upon his shoulders whether he will or not. The result is perhaps the most profound work of literary criticism on historical principles by any modern American with the possible exception of Lowes's *Road to Xanadu.*

The association of the titles of these two books here is not an accident. The training and equipment of the two authors is similar

New York: Oxford University Press, 1941. Reviewed in (1) *Saturday Review of Literature* 24 (June 14, 1941): 6., and (2) *American Literature* 13 (January 1941): 432-435.

in kind and degree, the problems with which they deal both arise from Coleridge's organic theory of the imagination, and the methods of their criticism are kindred. The subjects alone are markedly different. Both books are evidences of what happens when long hours of research of the traditional objective sort are fused and ignited by the critical imagination. It seems strange that Mr. Matthiessen, in acknowledging so frankly his indebtedness, has not mentioned this work of his colleague.

American Renaissance is a book with a thesis supported by an overwhelming mass of selected and interpreted evidence. But because its author keeps his thesis malleable and carefully avoids dogmatism, it would not be fair to tie it down to a single statement. Brooks, Mumford, and others have pointed out that American culture in some mysterious way flowered during the short period 1850-55, mainly though not exclusively in New England. Mr. Matthiessen sets himself the task of analyzing that flowering by a close examination of the works of five major authors who during that period issued a part of their most profound and characteristic work. He establishes two chief poles of reference: Coleridge's *Aids to Reflection,* the American edition of which appeared in 1829, and T. S. Eliot's *Selected Essays, 1917-1932,* perhaps the most influential of contemporary literary criticisms. Looking forward from Coleridge, he traces the direct impact of the organic theory on Emerson, Thoreau, and Whitman, and its derivative effect in the development of a theory of tragedy by Hawthorne and Melville. Looking backward from Eliot, he sees his American Renaissance in the light of the metaphysical poetry of the seventeenth century and its antecedents in Shakespeare and the Elizabethans. From these two poles, his lines of critical investigation move, in terms of dominant themes, inward to a detailed analysis of a dozen or more books by five American authors, in themselves and in relationship to each other, their authors, and their backgrounds, and outward to the limits of cultural history from ancient Greece to modern America.

There is no single conclusion that can be drawn from this mass of evidence, much of it subjective, and its critical synthesis and interpretation. The scholar may be most impressed by the first ambitious application of a current theory of historical criticism, the specialist by the new knowledge of the writings of one or more of the authors concerned. For example, this is the first full and accurate record of the friendship between Hawthorne and Melville, and corrects, by an examination of Melville's markings in his own copies of Hawthorne's books, the erroneous impressions left by Mumford's treatment of the problem.

For the reader who is not concerned with such technical questions, the book presents at least one important lesson: that even in our short century and a half of national existence, we have created a native myth of the democratic man, capable of all the range of experience of truth and error, good and evil, of the traditional heroic man, and that American literature has at least once explored and expressed the eternal verities of that myth. In a time of crisis this is the sort of assurance that we need.

REVIEW 2

I have already reviewed Mr. Matthiessen's book elsewhere in general terms. I should like here to consider its importance as a contribution to American literary history and to the theory and technique of historical writing. Even though its method is non-chronological, *American Renaissance* seems to me to be an important piece of historical writing, and should influence our concepts of how the history of American literature might be rewritten.

First, what Mr. Matthiessen is not: He is not a passive, objective chronicler. Events pass before his review weighted by values and in interrelationships other than juxtaposition. He has conceived his problem as a whole, established his own attitude toward it, and exercised his critical judgment as well as his historical knowledge at every point in the selection and arrangment of material for discussion.

Second, he is not a social or intellectual historian in the strict uses of those terms. His interest in plan and pattern in the affairs of men is based on neither sociological nor philosophical grounds. The plane of his thought and writing is that of art and culture, and past movements in social and philosophical forces are reduced to a secondary plane to be treated, as they should be fully treated in literary history, as causal and consequential factors. There is not here the confusion between literary and other forms of history that one finds in those historians who evaluate literature in terms of its content of communism, agrarian democracy, Puritanism, materialistic determinism, or other borrowed -isms. The central pole of reference is aesthetic significance.

But he has not, on the other hand, reduced literature to pure expression by divorcing form from content and treating it in a vacuum, as belletristic critics did in an earlier day and the post-neohumanists sometimes attempt to do today. He revives from Coleridge and Emerson an organic theory of literary composition and, while keeping his emphasis upon expression, gives full and qualitative consideration to the thing expressed in its relationship to its form, developing a modern functionalism in literary criticism.

The key to his method is given in the opening sentence of his preface: "The starting point for this book was my realization of how great a number of our past masterpieces were produced in one concentrated moment of expression." This was the five years following 1850, the distillation point in our literary history for the expression of the first American man, i.e., the emotionally and intellectually mature product of the thirteen original colonies. His economic being was the result of an expanding agrarianism; his spiritual and intellectual being, of the breakdown of Puritanism into cool Unitarianism and fervent Transcendentalism; his social and political being, of his traditional devotion to the ideals and possibilities of democracy. Here are the three background books which Mr. Matthiessen was prepared to write, but he wrote none of them; his is a literary history. Adopting Ezra Pound's thesis that "the history of art is the history of masterwork, not of failures or mediocrity," he continues, "My aim has been to follow these books [the mid-nineteenth-century American masterworks] through their implications, to observe them as the culmination of their authors' talents, to assess them in relationship to one another and to the drift of our literature since, and, so far as possible, to evaluate them in accordance with the enduring requirements for great art."

The statement of a theory of literary history is easier than its application to a specific problem. Mr. Matthiessen deals with his by four full-length studies of the work of Emerson, Hawthorne, Melville, and Whitman, respectively. In the first, Emerson, with the assistance of Thoreau, states the metaphysical and ethical ideals of life in America, and the organic theory of its expression. In the second, Hawthorne, artist and skeptic, reveals the difficulties of the artist in this situation without resolving them. His acceptance of evil in the world, even though he could not envision an evil world, opened the paths of tragedy, escape and despair and so prepared for Melville, James, and Eliot. In the third, Melville confronts the dualism in life which Emerson sought to distill to a single essence and Hawthorne, in fright, to veil thinly. Art must accept the primitive depths of nature as well as the "refined ascent of the mind." In his acceptance of the whole of experience he recalls Shakespeare, as he does in his development of original comic and tragic art forms. But he is finally an "American Hamlet," his conflict, like Hawthorne's, unresolved. In the fourth, Whitman, at his best, succeeds in bridging the void by "making the specific richly symbolic of the universal." His confident vision "led him to fulfill the most naive and therefore most natural kind of romanticism for America, the romanticism of the future." The relationship of this vision and its expression to later American poetry (e.g. E. A. Robinson and Sandburg) and painting (e.g. Eakins and Henri) is effectively noted.

The central quesiton of the book is adequately answered; satisfactory explanations are given for the concentration of art expression in the middle years of the last century; even though at times condensation would make the reader's progress easier and the writer's points sharper. The larger framework of the book, which involves the seventeenth-century English metaphysical poets, Coleridge and European romanticism, passages from the history of American painting, and T. S. Eliot and modern metaphysicians, serves its purpose of high-lighting the American romantic movement, but is in itself somewhat eclectic and fortuitous, the product rather of Mr. Matthiessen's own intellectual equipment than of inevitable and organic relationship to the main study.

These are necessary weaknesses of the method, as no critic can be omniscient. They can be accepted as long as the book is merely a critical analysis of one problem in a literary history rather than an attempt to deal with that history as a whole. But a modification of the method to make it more generally applicable may well serve as a substantial platform for the reconsideration of the complete story of American letters. The emphasis upon masterworks as the primary material of literary history; the ability to remain on the plane of art and culture while giving full weight to the causal significance of social and intellectual forces; and the sense of pattern in past events, provide an historical method for other special studies like this as well as for the more ambitious attack upon the whole problem, which must sooner or later be made.

18

1941

○ THE INTENT OF THE ARTIST ○
by Sherwood Anderson, Thornton Wilder,
Roger Sessions, and William Lescaze,
edited by Augusto Santino,

○ THE INTENT OF THE CRITIC ○
by Edmund Wilson, Norman Foerster,
John Crowe Ransom, and W. H. Auden,
edited by Donald Stauffer

A symposium is always a useful instrument for bringing diverse thought and activity into focus. Edmund Wilson's essay on literary history gave me much perspective on my own thinking and made me realize that my ultimate source might be Vico, whom I had never studied; and he helped me to distinguish the essential contributions of Marx and Freud from the misuses made of them by stereotyped communism and psychoanalysis. But the essay itself was disappointing to me because Wilson was a historical critic and not, as I was becoming, a literary historian. I have organized many symposia, and I recognize these two books as among the most helpful in an agitated and productive period in American aesthetic and historical learning.

Princeton: Princeton University Press, 1941. Reviewed in *American Literature* 14 (March 1942): 97-98.

The assembling of two symposia on the arts is a worthy but a discouraging task, for a symposium is presumably to be judged by its success in discovering a diversity and then reconciling it into at least a firm framework of unity. In the subjects of these two books, diversity is not difficult to discover. Their success in establishing rational unities is more dubious.

Let it be said first that the artist, however much he may protest that his allegiance is to an impersonal social or philosophical ideal, is inescapably an individual, and that the process of creation in art tends to develop rather than to suppress his individuality. Nor is the critic of art exempt from these necessities, for he must partake of the character and function of the artist or he is temperamentally alienated from his material. If this principle be questioned, the substance of these two volumes would provide sufficient documentation, and there is no noticeable difference on this point between the two. Even those contributors like Norman Foerster, John Crowe Ransom, Thornton Wilder, and Roger Sessions, who most nearly approach the impersonal and objective in their theories, are in their own writing intense individualists.

The aim of rational unity in a symposium on art is foredoomed to failure. In spite of the parallel titles and similar quartering of the proposed problems of the two volumes, no two contributors use the same or kindred styles, start from the same or related premises, organize their material on one pattern, or reach conclusions which are at all comparable. In the first, Mr. Wilson presents a cursory history of his own brand of historical criticism, Mr. Foerster earnestly argues for an ethical substance in judgment, Mr. Ransom constructs an exposition of a self-contained critical method, and Mr. Auden persuades the reader that democracy is a healthier aesthetic climate than is fascism. In the second Mr. Anderson offers forty delightful pages on how it feels to be Mr. Anderson, Mr. Wilder lays down a few crisp rules for the construction of a play, Mr. Sessions makes understandable the transition from primitive to sophisticated music, and Mr. Lescaze, in Socratic mood, convinces a mythical "Fred" that functionalism in architecture is a creed worthy of propagation for the health of our national life. Messrs. Centeno and Stauffer in each contribute a stimulating fifth paper in which, among speculations of their own, they hint at the framework which was constructed by the originators of these symposia and rather weakly indicate how their unruly brood might have behaved if they had not been artists. The reviewer, in spite of all this debate on law and order, is forced to the execrable form of impressionism in confession that he liked best Mr. Anderson's and Mr. Ransom's quite unlike contributions, that he was challenged most by Messrs. Lescaze and Auden, that he found Messrs. Foerster and Sessions a bit on the heavily academic side, and that Messrs. Wilson and Wilder seemed quite convincing but a bit thin.

For their diversity, therefore, these books offer a genuine reward to anyone who has attempted to create or to think about art in any of its forms, and perhaps in this fact alone lies their unity. Individualism, as Goethe, Whitman, Shelley, and many another romantic has discovered, provides its own basis for unity, albeit on a somewhat mystical plane. The artist in his splendid isolation is brother to his fellow man insofar as the aesthetic experience is shared. These books prove, if nothing else, that the use of schools in art and in criticism lies not in their ability to formulate an aesthetic norm but in their power to prick the aesthetic consciousness until the red blood flows. Let us have more such symposia.

19

1941

✤ AMERICAN JOURNALISM: A HISTORY ✤ OF NEWSPAPERS IN THE UNITED STATES THROUGH 250 YEARS, 1690 TO 1940 by Frank Luther Mott

Frank Luther Mott, in contrast to Matthiessen, was a man of details and externals. Tireless in his accumulation of evidence, he revealed in his multivolume history of American magazines the avenues of communication that brought the new American writers into touch with their native and natural audiences. Of the many histories of American journalism, his was the most satisfactory because of this background. The newspaper is the first rung on the cultural ladder that climbs, if given time, to masterpieces of comedy and tragedy, realism and romance. The process repeated itself a thousand times as the frontier moved west and the local newspaper appeared and reappeared. Thus the history of the American newspaper is part of the foundation work for an understanding of the American literary masterpiece.

Among the many subliterary aspects of American literary history, newspaper journalism has already been granted a fair proportion of attention. Mr. Mott's is the sixth survey account of its dramatic and colorful development from Ben Harris's *Public Occurrences* of 1690 to the gargantuan *New York Times* of 1940. But no one of them has understood so fully the organic character of the news-

New York: The Macmillan Company, 1941. Reviewed in *American Literature* 15 (March 1943): 72-73.

paper nor has studied its growth with so rich a knowledge of the cultural soil from which it sprang. Fresh from his three[five]-volume *A History of American Magazines,* he has thrown together the new information which he collected incidentally to that study with the previously known facts, and has virtually tossed off a work which would have required years of analytical research on the part of anyone else. The result is a clear, exhaustive, and well-balanced account of a confusing problem.

His pattern for the main outlines of American journalism follows that of W. G. Bleyer, A. M. Lee, J. M. Lee, G. H. Payne and Frederic Hudson. There is the struggle to found newspapers in the Colonies; the political partisan press of the first half-century of independence; the penny press and personal journalism dominated by Horace Greeley and James Gordon Bennett; and the big-business press of Joseph Pulitzer and William Randolph Hearst. Mr. Mott's contributions are many nevertheless. Factually, they are most notable in the early years when newspapers and magazines are less clearly distinguished and his intimate knowledge of the latter can be fully used. He has also given careful attention to the press of the West and South, particularly of New Orleans, San Francisco, Chicago, and Atlanta, and has pointed up its relationships to that of the metropolitan centers of the Northeast. And in spite of the survey character of his work, the incidental importance of Ed Howe's *Atchison Globe,* William Allen White's *Emporia Gazette,* W. N. Byers's *Rocky Mountain News,* E. W. Scripps's *Chicago Day Book,* John Forney's *Philadelphia Press,* and of many other relatively minor journals is described succinctly and evaluated precisely. The death of the *Boston Transcript* and the birth of *PM* mark the end of his story, but Marshall Field's more recent Chicago experiments prove that there are still more chapters to be written.

It would be folly to call his book entertaining in the ordinary sense because only small sections of it can be absorbed at any one sitting and the text is chopped into segments of a paragraph or a page or two, but Mr. Mott has two qualities which make the term applicable for those who are not afraid of massed facts. These are his own enthusiasm for his subject and his impartiality. The newspaper world is a maze of paradoxes in which the villains are heroes and the heroes villains. Without sentimentality, he can make us love a Bennett or a Hearst in the same degree that Bret Harte can a John Oakhurst. His book is rooted in human nature and in the American faith in vitality as a way of life.

But the special value of the book lies in its contribution to American cultural history. Mr. Mott holds journalism in the prism of general culture at all times. He sees it in terms of politics, economics, religion, popular taste, international relations, personalities, and literature—although not as much of the latter as one might expect. Of all his many approaches to his subject, however, that as bibliographer is probably basic. Newspapers to him are in themselves living entities, as books are to the good bibliographer. Their paper, their presses, their circulation mechanisms, their types, their sizes are given relatively as full and careful study as are their editorial policies. This is sound method for any kind of cultural history. Other factors in American life, such as the theater, libraries, educational institutions, and copyright laws, should have similar three-dimensional treatment before we can fully understand ourselves.

20

1942

✌ THE ROOTS OF AMERICAN CULTURE ✌
by Constance Rourke

When Constance Rourke died in 1941 she was well embarked on what was to have been her major work, a history of American culture in three volumes based on the theory (which she owes largely to the German poet and philosopher of history Johann Gottfried Herder) that man is a part of nature and that his basic character is derived directly from his environment through intuition. This theory provided an explanation of national character, which freed it from both a formal aesthetic tradition and a political structure and sought to root it in the evolving folk and popular arts of any people in any given place and period of time.

Her earlier work, in addition to *American Humor* (review 8, pp. 24-26) had dealt with the naturalist J. J. Audubon, the frontiersman Davy Crockett, Henry Ward Beecher and P. T. Barnum, and the frontier actresses Lotta Crabtree, Adah Menken, and others—surely a motley company, but they had in common their closeness to the virgin American experience and the westward movement of the frontier. Her hope was to discover and define a distinctive American aesthetic, however crude, as the expression of an emerging American national character.

This is exactly what the editors of *Literary History of the United States* were looking for. Constance Rourke's contri-

New York: Harcourt, Brace and Company, 1942. Reviewed in *American Literature* 15 (March 1943): 77-79.

bution, however abortive, when added to those of Parrington, Jones, Matthiessen, and others, was central to the philosophy and architecture of that work. It was fitting that her friend Van Wyck Brooks, who started with the same questions and ended with almost diametrically opposite answers, should have undertaken to edit her fragments.

Constance Rourke did not live long enough to write her history of American culture. If she had, it might have been as important an influence in redirecting research as was Parrington's *Main Currents in American Thought.* Her underlying thesis, although totally different, was as clearly defined, as revolutionary, and as significant as was his, but she never accomplished more than its statement in theoretical form and its application in a series of sketches, the most sustained of which was her *American Humor.*

In the title essay of this posthumous collection, she challenges the conventional approach to research for its dependence on what Fiske has called the "transit of culture" theory. As she states it, this theory holds "that if we dipped deeply enough and often enough into the major European streams we might hope to witness their rise among us." She is undoubtedly correct in her charge that this theory was accepted in colonial times, was the chief motivation for our early national schools in literature, music, and the fine arts, and is still dominant in our thinking.

As a substitute she proposes a "configuration theory" which is based on Herder's concept of "folk-life as fundamental and his contention that the folk-arts laid a base for the fine arts." According to this theory, geographical, economic, and social factors provide a basic cultural pattern from which the arts develop together, rather than each for itself, by a process of "gradual enrichment." In order to discover the true nature of American culture, therefore, the scholar must seek his sources in the elementary motivation of the American people rather than in the influence of this or that person or book or school. This approach leads to an organic rather than a chronological sequence in literary history. It sees the rise of American culture in terms of basic needs that originate in the peculiar conditions of settlement on this continent, and it reveals a process of cultural evolution, often repeated and in its earlier stages frequently confused, but capable of clear definition and firm application. Her conclusions, if sound, are as important to the creative artist as to the historian of culture because they seek to establish a dynamic and autogenous American tradition, only now, approaching maturity. The task of the historian is to define this tradition more clearly by examining the most minute aspects of its origin and growth; that of the artist is to fall into its current with the conscious understanding provided by this investigation, and to give new and mature expression to it.

This thesis led Miss Rourke to a lifelong study of American folk arts, not for themselves but for what they might reveal toward a definition of American character in the abstract. Her work is not to be confused with that of the typical folklorist, whose main interest is usually antiquarian or naturalistic. For her, folk art is but one source; perhaps the most revealing because elementary, but only one of many. The work of Frank Lloyd Wright or Henry James, however, has the same kind of interest as has an Ephrata imprint, a Gold-Coast theatrical, or a Shaker songbook.

Her method of research was as consistent as her motivating theory. Because the field was huge and unexplored, her results were exceedingly spotty. But she completed studies of Audubon and Crockett as well as the very brief but revealing essays on obscure writers, minstrels, composers, painters, and religious sects which fill her last volume. Miscellaneous as these essays are, they have a firmly knit unity when related to her theory and to her method. Seldom has a never-to-be-written book been so thoroughly revealed in a few preliminary sketches.

The importance of her work lies not so much in its novelty as in the clarity of its challenge. The sources of both her theory and her method are not difficult to trace, but they will be found for the most part outside the fields of literature and art. Others like Mary Austin, Lewis Mumford, Van Wyck Brooks, Bernard DeVoto, Edward Wagenknecht, Carl Sandburg (surely a motley company!) have applied parts of her theory to significant studies. But no one has attempted as broad an application of the philosophical and sociological principles involved as has she.

An attack upon her position might begin with a denial of her biological premises. Man, it might be contended, does not continuously repeat the cycle of organic growth from the simple to the complex; the cultural stream flows through time without more than slight modifications wrought by place or era. Or the attack might be more specific: this theory places too much emphasis on the autogenous quality of American culture to the disregard of more ancient traditions; it merges the arts into one indistinguishable mass without due regard for the discriminations which civilized man has so carefully wrought between them.

It is to be hoped that such attacks may be made, but this is not the place to make them. Only by being combated can the full force of the theory be felt in literary and art history, and its influence is needed. The kind of research which Miss Rourke called for and started herself to do is demanded in order to bridge our ignorance of the sociological bases of art, particularly in the United States. She provides a new approach and a new technique for the study of American literature and the related arts and has made a major contribution toward the ripening of our civilization.

21

1942

ON NATIVE GROUNDS: AN INTERPRETATION OF MODERN AMERICAN PROSE-LITERATURE
by Alfred Kazin

By 1942 the main outlines of the new history of American literature had been drawn. The socioeconomic idiom of Parrington and others of the pioneers had proven itself as the basic structure, but it had also revealed its fatal weakness in its failure to recognize literature as art rather than as mere document and to deal with each artist as a unique sensibility. Matthiessen had made the correction for the Romantic period, and Rourke had found a new and more creative relationship than the mere socioeconomic in the growth of literature from the folk experience. Alfred Kazin's was a new voice when he wrote this book, but his concentration on the problem of the realist movement in American prose of more recent times did much to fill out the picture.

The central problem of Mr. Kazin's book is the search for reality which dominated the American literary mind at the close of the nineteenth century and up to the present. He proceeds to his task, as historian, of discovering the terms in which American writers sought reality during this period, the nature of the reality which they sought, and their varying degrees of success in the quest. His story falls readily into three parts: from Howells to Randolph Bourne and the early Van Wyck Brooks (1890-1917); the war generation, from Sherwood Anderson to John Dos Passos (1918-1929); and the

New York: Reynal and Hitchcock, 1942, Reviewed in *American Literature* 15 (November 1943): 303-305.

recent past, from J. T. Farrell to the documentary films of Pare Lorentz (1930-1940).

The writers of the first period failed of their goal because theirs was a literature of enmity and protest, of uncertainty that led from muckraking to debunking. The acquisitive instinct in society was at war during this period with the creative instinct in the artist, yet the conflict was a necessary step in the artist's process of understanding his grounds. These writers lived "on the periphery of one moral and intellectual revolution after another, and finally built their creative understanding on fragments" (p. 164).

In the second period, the new freedom won by the liberal critics at such cost seemed on the verge of discovering a positive formula for reality, but the hope evaporated in the dismay of postwar disillusionment and depression. In the third period, a new realism, built upon the old, gradually rose out of the morass with the aid of the tragic sense of recognition, a painful realization of "the long and deep estrangement of the modern American writer from his society" (p. 469).

When William Dean Howells moved from Boston to New York in 1885, the history of modern American literature began. There have been many attempts to tell this story, but none of them has been wholly successful. Nor should it be expected that a genuine historical perspective can be achieved for the half century of any immediate past.

Mr. Kazin has been relatively more successful than others because he has made a precise and accurate distinction between literary and other forms of cultural or social history, and because he keeps in mind the liberal tradition of American democracy, the tradition of a society founded upon the Bill of Rights, as his ideological framework.

"I have never been able to understand," he states in his preface, "why the study of literature in relation to society should be divorced from a full devotion to what literature is in itself." Literature is "produced by a succession of individuals and out of individual sensibility and knowledge and craft." An American literature must therefore be built "on native grounds," it must express the success or failure of the American writer in expressing the experience of the free individual in a democracy. Starting with a thesis which seems at first glance to be the contrary of the folk theory of Constance

Rourke, he reaches a conclusion which is strikingly similar to hers: that the American writer must come to terms with his environment rather than by an imposition upon it of ideas and forms which are not essentials of its being. Both are right, and there is no ultimate conflict between the two views.

Little of this historical framework can be seriously questioned, yet it has never before been so broadly stated and so clearly explained. These are obviously the things that happened. It requires no warping of the material to illustrate them.

Trouble arises only when the historian turns critic, as he must if he is to fulfill his full obligation. This Mr. Kazin does with dogged and not always dispassionate courage. To call him a Fascist when he attacks Communism and the writers of the Left is to read only selected pages of his book or to read the whole with jaundiced eye. He attacks the Marxist school of American writers, but he appreciates the historical importance of Marx. He also attacks the Freudians, the Hitlerites, the Capitalists, the Progressives, and every other group which substitutes loyalty to the party line for the free exercise of the artist's creative imagination. But he praises John Dos Passos, Van Wyck Brooks, Thomas Wolfe, and others, conservative, liberal, or radical, when he is convinced that their quest for reality is sincere in intention and relatively successful as art. The distinction becomes altogether clear in such a case as that of James T. Farrell, who is recognized as "perhaps the most powerful naturalist who ever worked in the American tradition" (p. 381), but who, with all his "powerful and vital art," is "a perfect example of that unconscious and benevolent philistinism which believes that one escapes from materialism by surrendering to it" (p. 385).

With all its general excellences, the book is more than normally uneven in its individual judgments and in its style. Both are of high quality at their best, but personal prejudices and taste too often destroy otherwise illuminating analyses, a tone of sophomoric irony too often defeats the objectivity of an estimate, and a sentimental enthusiasm or dislike too often creates a turgid and overwrought style. But none of these faults are serious; they are only annoying. The book stands as a serious and successful essay in genuine literary history, even though the sensitive reader of modern American literature may feel the impulse to throw it out the window at least a dozen times.

22

1944

✿ THE SHAPE OF BOOKS TO COME ✿
by J. Donald Adams

As editor of the *New York Times Book Review* for many years, J. Donald Adams was the last faint echo of that group of critics—Alden, Stedman, Stoddard, Gilder—who dominated the New York literary scene in the closing years of the last century by control of its major monthly magazines, *Harper's, Scribner's,* and *Century.* Willard Thorp has called them "Defenders of Ideality" in the *Literary History of the United States* with their basic tenet that the real is sordid and a sweet and pure idealism should be the primary aim of literature. Adams was actually speaking rather of the shape of books that had gone than of books to come.

With an increasing emphasis on the teaching of American literature in our schools and colleges, it becomes important to define the critical philosophy by which we should judge contemporary writers. The task is never easy, because the nearness of the material makes perspective hard to establish.

The conventional view of modern American writers is that those who are not depressing are unimportant. That this view is completely erroneous does not seem to matter. We pull a long face and read about the degenerates in Steinbeck's *Cannery Row* without realizing that we are supposed to chuckle; because it is sordid, it must be great. We greet *Forever Amber* as relatively important

---

New York: Viking Press, 1944. Reviewed in *College English* 6 (April 1945): 417-418.

because it spends some six hundred pages of shoddy writing on a group of low and dissolute people in high places. We treasure Hemingway's *For Whom the Bell Tolls* as a classic because it invokes a noble theme from a long-dead poet and deals "realistically" with a modern civil war. These are bad judgments that mix the great with the shoddy because they are based on a false assumption. The sordid is not necessarily the real, and the real is not necessarily the great.

Mr. Adams lays the foundation for his study of twentieth-century literature on a contrary assumption. He turns for authority to those writers "who did not flinch from the observation and recording of human folly, stupidity, and viciousness, but who could still hold to a belief in the indestructible dignity of the human spirit, in the resolution and hope by which it has endured." In Theodore Dreiser's *An American Tragedy* he sees the culmination of a literary movement based on a biochemical view of life and preaching a fundamentally false theory of inevitability; and in John Hersey's *A Bell for Adano* he finds that "flash of illumination" and that "current of human sympathy and understanding" which are essential to great writing. With these poles of reference, he ranges Robert Frost, Elizabeth Madox Roberts, Ellen Glasgow, and Willa Cather on the side of the angels; the early Hemingway, Thomas Wolfe, and William Faulkner on the contrary side. For Sinclair Lewis, Scott Fitzgerald, the later Hemingway, John Steinbeck, H. L. Davis, and many others he finds a middle ground. Furthermore, he attempts to prove that American literature is moving away from the sordid and despairing philosophy of the early years of the century and that "the shape of books to come" will be determined by a renewed faith in human nature.

It would be pleasant to accept this thesis in toto as does Van Wyck Brooks's Oliver Allston, Howard Mumford Jones in some of his moods, and an increasing body of contemporary critics. The great literature of the past would seem to validate it in principle. But Mr. Adams, like many another, falls into a critical error which distorts many of his judgments and leads to overenthusiasm for much that is merely sentimental and shallow. He asks not only that a writer have a deep concern for human values but that he preach a gospel of sweetness and light. He does not recognize, as does Amos Wilder in his more profound book on a similar topic, *The Spiritual*

Aspects of Modern Poetry (1940), that much of the literature of confidence "is wholesome but not whole" and that such earnest seekers as Wolfe, Jeffers, Eliot, and even Faulkner are "wrestling with ethical issues and value issues" as sincerely as were Shakespeare in his tragic period or Voltaire in *Candide*.

The judgment of the future may well hold that the great writers of this period through which we are living are those who in their despair have rediscovered man's basic needs rather than those who have cheerfully re-expressed his faith. The sordid and realistic writers fall easily into two groups: those who are profoundly moved by the tragic plight or the comic necessities of human nature in the modern world and those who are merely sensationalists. Dreiser, Wolfe, Jeffers, Steinbeck, and some of Hemingway fall into the first; some of Hemingway, Cain, some of Faulkner, and some of Caldwell fall into the second. The old assumption that the real is sordid and the sordid is great must go; but our writers must find a morality which rests on something more profound than Major Joppolo's naive faith if we are to rediscover an ethical standard for literary judgment. Mr. Adams serves as a useful corrective for the false and shallow critical standards of some of his opponents, but his own position is equally warped by ethical standards which are too shallow and too formalized.

23

1945

LA LITTÉRATURE AMÉRICAINE
by Charles Cestre

Professor Charles Cestre of the Sorbonne, the first scholar to hold a chair of American literature in France, had learned about his subject from the older and more traditional books in American literary history. He reflected mainly the "genteel" point of view discussed in my review of *The Shape of Books to Come* above and was little influenced by the newer trends in either literature or scholarship. His presence in his high academic post was more important for the opportunity it created for his successors than for anything he himself contributed to the changing philosophy of literary history. The phenomenal spread of American studies throughout European universities was a much later development.

Now that undue deference to British opinion of American literature is a thing of the past, the growing interest of Continental critics in our literature becomes a matter of note. The mature judgment of the retired Professor of American Civilization at the Sorbonne should command attention. But Charles Cestre's little book is informed rather than profound. It reflects the critical perspective of the elder generation of American scholars rather than that of the great French critics; more of Matthews, Parrington, Quinn, and Foerster than of Sainte-Beuve, Brunetière, or Anatole France. It is America speaking to France rather than France to America.

The basically French character of this "introduction à la littéra-

---

Paris: Librairie Armand Colin, 1945. Reviewed in *American Literature* 18 (January 1947): 335-336.

ture américaine" for French readers is apparent only in its reliance on the "genre" as a system of organization for historical facts. Cestre sees two tendencies at war in our literary history: that of romance and that of realism. With the excesses of both he has little sympathy, even in the cases of such French favorites as Cooper, Poe, Whitman, or Mark Twain. He prefers the "health" of Irving, Howells, or Edith Wharton to the violence of Melville, Dreiser, or Hemingway. In Emerson's and Robinson's blends of romance and realism he finds our highest achievement: themes born of American life but transformed by imagination into symbols of the life of the spirit. With Gallic detachment, he shapes the course of our literary history about this aesthetic ideal.

The result is not an unhappy one, even though it serves better for the treatment of those writers whose places have already been reserved for them in the literary hierarchy than as a measure of stature for recent writers. From Parrington and other political and social historians, Cestre has absorbed enough knowledge of American life and ideas to provide an autogenous background for his literary judgments. He does not overvalue Longfellow, and he gives Dreiser adequate historical treatment. Mark Twain he slights rather badly, but the analysis of Henry Adams, though superficial, is in good proportion. The intrinsic excellence of Stephen Crane is totally missed and that of Emily Dickinson scantily recognized; whereas Marion Crawford, Booth Tarkington, and Branch Cabell are perhaps allowed more than their rightful space. Too many recent writers are discussed for so rapid a survey, and critical perspective becomes increasingly murky as the twentieth century is approached. Of the generation following that of Sherwood Anderson and E. A. Robinson, he has almost no knowledge, and the book concludes with a rather confused review of "divers vents d'esprit," arranged according to literary types.

Since its purpose is merely to introduce American literature to French readers, this rapid review can therefore serve a useful end without serious distortion of either truth or values. It is reasonably accurate and its judgments are mild. But for American readers it can be of little service. There is much work still to be done by the younger foreign students—of whom there are increasing numbers—in interpreting American history and literature both to their own peoples and to us.

24

1948

✺ THE RISE OF THE AMERICAN NOVEL ✺
by Alexander Cowie

It was inevitable that once the main outlines of American literary history had been drawn on the new model, histories of the major literary types or genres would follow, but Cowie did little more than assemble the materials for a history of the novel, built about his own personal interests and enthusiasms.

The temptation to write an unfavorable review of this book is great, but fortunately it is offset by the impulse to be enthusiastic about its author's enthusiasms. For this is not a literary history in the conventional sense, and it seems to have no clear procedure of its own other than that of the running commentary.

Mr. Cowie explains in his preface that his intention is rather more critical than historical, that he wishes to "indicate the evolution of the American novel by means of comparatively full treatments of representative writers," both major and minor. But he never makes clear why this writer is selected and that omitted, or what each represents. Sometimes contemporary vogue seems to be the test, sometimes intrinsic excellence, sometimes significant comment on American life. The treatments themselves vary not only in length but in method, as though written at widely separated times. Some give full biographical data and some almost none; some summarize plots in detail and some note merely the central theme; in some the novelist's

New York: The American Book Co., 1948. Reviewed in *Saturday Review of Literature* 31 (June 26, 1948): 19.

philosophy is discussed and in some it is ignored. And—to complete the catalogue of faults in order to dispose of them—the writing itself varies from succinct and revealing comment to vague and repetitious commentary, from tight and effective sentences to a style so loose and incorrect that the veteran teacher of composition cries out for the blue pencil.

But with these things said and the conscience thereby cleared, the critic can relax and enjoy the high spirits and the genuine enthusiasm for his books that Mr. Cowie has maintained for more than a decade of preparation and more than seven hundred pages of print. His book was apparently planned as a companion volume to Harry Hartwick's *Foreground of American Fiction,* issued by the same publisher back in 1934, for he stops with the writers of the Nineties, where Hartwick takes up the story. Mr. Cowie's task was by far the greater and he took time to read afresh not only the novels he planned to discuss but most of the critical commentary available on them and their authors. He obviously enjoyed the stupendous task he set himself. The result is an informed and discriminating account of American novels and novelists by a reader who enjoys a good story at the same time that he is critical of its shortcomings, and who is able to communicate both his enjoyment and his criticism.

Because he is interested mainly in the gift of story-telling, Mr. Cowie is best when his author is most highly endowed with that gift. Brockden Brown and Cooper fare best of the early writers, Howells of the later ones; and among the minor writers, those who, like John Neal and George Lippard, write with unrestrained zest receive their full but belated recognition. The more intellectual novelists like Hawthorne, Melville, and Henry James are given careful and courteous attention only. The chapter on Melville is little more than an account of how his work was received by the critics and the public; those on Hawthorne and James are fair and objective appraisals without much conviction of greatness.

Perhaps this reviewer has succumbed to his temptation and written an unfavorable review after all. If so, it was not his intention. There are few literary histories that give pleasure in the reading, and this is one of the few. Mr. Cowie's lack of dogmatism and his faith in his own responses make this book an invitation to learning, even though it is neither the first nor the last word on the subject.

25

1948

✣ THE THEORY OF ✣
AMERICAN LITERATURE
by Howard Mumford Jones

Howard Mumford Jones was one of the three scholars that
Henry Canby summoned to his comfortable home in Killingworth, Connecticut, to plan for a new literary history when
the Modern Language Association project for a multivolume
history to be prepared officially by the American Literature
Group was tabled at 1940 Cambridge meeting (the others
were Stanley Williams and myself). I have told this story in
some detail in my essay, "History of a History," which is
reprinted in this volume (pp. 111-127). At that conference all
of us agreed that such a history should and could be undertaken immediately, but no one of us was at the moment caught
up by the lure of taking the primary initiative. Jones joined
our editorial board later as an "associate," but he remained
throughout the "gadfly" as he called himself and, with his
infinite learning and incurable cynicism, helped the rest of us
maintain a humanistic perspective in the decade of aborning
of *Literary History of the United States.*

In the Messenger lectures at Cornell University in December
1947, his approach was much more positive and constructive.
The Theory of American Literature is more history than theory,
but he bases his account on the general point of view that I
hope has been evolving in the foregoing reviews and so writes

---

Ithaca, New York: Cornell University Press, 1948. Reviewed in *Saturday Review of
Literature* 32 (March 5, 1949): 32.

the first attempt at a systematic history of the movement. Although in some of his lectures and writings, Howard Jones has been tempted by the comforting sunshine of the "genteel tradition," in this book he threw his lot in with the mainstream of thinking in the field and gave source and shape to what has been called "the American literary history movement."

In six lectures, delivered at Cornell in December 1947, Howard Mumford Jones of Harvard attempted a historical review of the theories held by Americans about their own literary tradition from colonial times to the present. Even revised and documented for print, so ambitious an undertaking could hope only to be provocative rather than definitive; yet this book defines much. It advances definitions of literature in general and of the civilization of the United States in particular, and it develops a theory for the ideal history of our literature which must reveal the relationships between these two factors. The editorial connection of Mr. Jones with the new cooperative *Literary History of the United States* adds pertinence and zest to his analysis.

Mr. Jones's theory of literature rests firmly on the concept of the work of art as an immediate product of the time and place of its creation and of the race and personality of its creator. To Taine and his followers, he owes his emphasis on time, race, and environment; to Sainte-Beuve and Arnold his emphasis on the personality of the author. The problem of the literary historian is therefore the problem of the relationship of literature to the society which produces it. He sees the encyclopedic humanism of Bacon, Bouterwek, and Hallam modified by the dynamic discrimination of Goethe, De Staël, Sismondi, Schlegel, Cousin and Villemain, with their more romantic views of cultural setting. Not only does Mr. Jones advance this as his own theory, but he successfully demonstrates a constant and dominant influence of this view on American thinking about literature and literary history throughout our national life, developing by modification rather than fundamental change with the changing views of society advanced by nineteenth- and twentieth-century science.

The first stage in this development was the nationalist argument of the period 1815-1850, when the theory produced many controversial essays but only one literary history, that of Samuel Knapp (1829); but it nevertheless "laid the intellectual foundations upon which the structure of Moses Coit Tyler's histories was to be erected." In the period 1850-1924, the racist argument led to Anglophilism by ignoring the other factors in Taine's formula, time and environment; but of its three major literary histories, only Wendell's was completely anti-nationalist, Richardson's mildly so, and Tyler's squarely in the nationalist tradition. By 1924, the renewed quest for a "usable past" had been revived by the *Cambridge History,* Foerster's *Reinterpretation,* and Macy's *Spirit of American Literature,* and was clearly the main line of our thinking. By 1947, it had produced a group of literary histories of limited ideologies— Parrington, Calverton, and Lewisohn—and a vast accumulation of special studies, but no major history of American literature of broader scope. The stage was clearly set for an answer to Pattee's "Call for a Literary Historian" of 1924.

The strength of Mr. Jones's argument lies in its emphasis upon the continuing tradition of an American cultural nationalism which is dynamic rather than chauvinistic. Within the scope of his lectures, this is all that could be accomplished, and what he says desperately needed to be said. The weakness in his position lies in its failure to recognize that the nationalist theory, by its subordination of art to society, fails to take account of aesthetic factors and therefore cannot fully explain the two periods of genuine literary accomplishment in our history, the "American Renaissance" of 1850-55, and the present; nor can it do justice to such "un-American" Americans as Poe, James, and Eliot. Both terms of an equation such as that of art and society must be defined before the problem can be resolved, and the mutation in American aesthetic theory does not lie within the scope of this rapid survey except as an implied foil to the main argument. Only a design for a literary history which is broad enough to include impartially the concept of literature as timeless art as well as the concept of literature as social expression could come near to meeting the need that is here so lucidly and forcefully expressed.

26

1950

THE BEGINNINGS OF NATURALISM IN AMERICAN FICTION, 1891-1903
by Lars Aahnebrink

In the spring of 1950, when I was Fulbright Visiting Professor of American Literature at the University of Oslo, Norway, I received a call from Professor Liljegren of the University of Uppsala, Sweden, inviting me to be First Opponent at the doctor's oral of my friend Lars Aahnebrink. Lars, with his wife Erna, had been our paying house guests the previous winter in Swarthmore when both were in the United States on fellowships. The dissertation under review was, I believe, the first major work to be submitted for a doctorate in American literature in any Scandinavian country, and the occasion was one of the highest academic and international import. Aahnebrink survived my two hours of public questioning, won the prize for the best dissertation of the year, entertained all concerned with dinner and speeches into the early hours of the morning, and was appointed to the chair of American literature at his university.

Professional jealousies and an early death soon ended a promising career but, with the development of the American Institute under Sigmund Skard in Oslo and the establishment of American lectureships in the four leading Swedish Universities, the work of this day was not lost.

"Essays on American Language and Literature," ed. S. B. Liljegren, No. IX. Upsala 1950. Reviewed in *Moderna Språk* (1950): 103-105.

My review was written at Professor Liljegren's request and may reflect some of the excitement of the occasion. Needless to say, Aahnebrink shows the influence of the newer trends in American literary history in his emphasis on realism and naturalism, as well as deference to the demands of traditional philological scholarship in his efforts to assign specific European sources to individual American authors.

An inaugural dissertation for the degree of doctor of philosophy is often a factual contribution to knowledge upon which the candidate rests his hope for academic respectability and preferment in his profession. It is refreshing therefore to see a work of the scope and challenge of Dr. Aahnebrink's study of the beginnings of American naturalism presented for public defense. A more controversial subject could hardly be discovered and a more experimental method of dealing with it adopted.

This ambitious book is distinguished rather for its pioneering work in defining a large field of study than for its factual treatment of any one aspect of its subject. The questions it raises are more important to scholarship than are the answers it gives. Objection will be taken to it on many points, but in the end it should take its place as an inaugural work in the Swedish academic study of American literary history rather than as merely the inaugural work of a single scholar. Upon receipt of *Leaves of Grass* from a then unknown author, Emerson wrote to Whitman, "I greet you at the beginning of a great career." This is all he could be sure of when confronted with a volume which so defied precedent. In this case also one can be sure only that tradition has been violated and leadership asserted.

The book is really three closely related essays in interpretation of a complex problem the core of which is the part played by European literary forces in America's battle of the 1890s against a tradition of romantic respectability in her literature. Between 1880 and 1910 American fiction went through a violent upheaval. The three major writers of the time—Howells, Mark Twain and Henry James—all bear the scars of the conflict but are too individualistic to represent the main force in the movement. To understand the movement as a whole one must turn, as Dr. Aahnebrink has done, to lesser writers like Garland, Crane and Norris, and to experimental realists who preceded them. In these writers we discover the sources of much of the power and freedom of Dreiser, Hemingway, Faulkner, Wolfe, Steinbeck, and the modern school in American fiction in general. American fiction in that period learned to share—and even to lead— the cultural growth of Western Europe as a whole. It turned from a narrowly British to a more cosmopolitan and at the same time a less dependent relationship with other literatures. Dr. Aahnebrink has attempted to bring into a single work his studies of the beginnings of this movement in America, of the novels and short stories of its three leaders, and of the comparative European and American trends. The result, although somewhat diffuse, is the best general synthesis now available of the scholarship in this field.

The first section of the study builds upon MS sources in the USA, especially the Garland papers in Los Angeles, upon special studies of individual authors and general surveys of literary trends, and upon the texts of the authors themselves, to reveal Garland, Crane and Norris simultaneously in two apparently different contexts. Their work is but a small part of the main movement of American fiction of their time toward the portrayal of American life in literature. With the closing of the frontier and the challenge of the new science, the USA had at last become a major nation and it needed a new and more profoundly interpretative literature. The realist-naturalist movement was therefore a native and indigenous movement. But, as this study so brilliantly reveals, it developed striking parallels in theme and method with the similar movement in France, Russia, Scandinavia and Germany. In a series of six chapters, which do not follow logically the one from the other, Dr. Aahnebrink presents the main facts of this duplex problem by supplying in each chapter a different angle of attack on the main issue. The result is impressionistic rather than definitive, but it serves its purpose in placing the three authors in the dual contexts of the movement at home and abroad.

The study then moves on to a closer analysis of the texts of the fiction of the three authors within the period chosen for concentrated study. Here again the chapters are clustered about the problem, but the workmanship becomes considerably tighter. Chapters VII-IX inclusive show the philosophy and methods of the three experimental Americans to have much in common. Both the technical and thematic analyses serve the purpose of revealing a literary movement in an early and formative stage. Discussions of the problems of free will, sex, the beast in man, man's relationship to the modern universe, and the new woman, could each of them provide enough material for the ordinary dissertation, yet in each case the author has defined the problem closely and adduced enough material to place it in his study as a whole.

In his third section, Chapters X-XIV inclusive, the author finally comes to grips with the most difficult and important question in his study: How much did these Americans actually owe to Zola, Huysmans, Turgenev, Tolstoy, Ibsen, and incidentally to other European authors? Troubled by the lack of external evidence except in a few cases, he adopts a method of attributing influence wherever he finds strong parallels in theme, content, or technique. Used with extreme caution this method may reveal much, and one may agree with many of the conclusions reached in this study without accepting the validity of a large part of the so-called evidence it offers. The difficulty comes from the effort to super-impose the Germanic fetish-worship of sources upon the Gallic awareness of a climate of ideas in civilization. This is not the place to debate so large a problem of method in literary scholarship. But the problem must be debated further before broad and important questions such as that which is here raised can be dealt with in anything like finality. One lays down this monograph with a greatly increased understanding of the common literary drives in Europe and America during the second half of the 19th century. But at the same time one has a feeling that the problem has been grossly over-simplified in the effort to be conclusive on specific points. But conclusive on these or any other major points it has not been—nor could have been. The subject itself is too new and too complex for any final treatment yet.

27

1951

THE CONFIDENT YEARS, 1885-1915
by Van Wyck Brooks

Our old friend Van Wyck Brooks comes in again to help conclude our story. One of the most experienced and articulate of the twentieth-century literary commentators, his escape into a "usable past" had brought him into confrontation with his usable present. *Literary History of the United States* had been out four years when this book appeared, but it did not carry his name. He was invited to do a chapter on modern criticism, but he declined. He was right, because he had to conclude his study of what he once described to me as a "history of the literary life in America," which is not quite the same as literary history, and he could not shift his theoretical ground to deal with problems from our point of view.

With this study of his own times, Van Wyck Brooks announces the completion of what he now calls, "Makers and Finders: A History of the Writer in America, 1800-1915." It is now possible to apply to the life work of one of the major literary figures of our time the classic questions of criticism: What has the writer proposed to himself to do? How far has he succeeded in carrying out his own plan? But this is a review; and only a few stammering remarks can be made. Look elsewhere and much later for the final estimate.

As with the Leather-Stocking Tales of an earlier student of an even earlier American past the recommended order of reading of

---

New York: E. P. Dutton & Co., 1951. Reviewed in *Saturday Review of Literature* 35 (January 5, 1952): 11-12.

these five books differs from that of the writing. *The World of Washington Irving* is first in chronological order; then follow *The Flowering of New England* (still the best of the series), *The Times of Melville and Whitman, New England: Indian Summer,* and finally the present volume. But anyone who has watched Mr. Brooks spin his web during the past ten and more years will still prefer to read the books as they were written, for, like the industrious spider, the chronicler of America's literary past has proceeded from the core of meaning outward with cunning accuracy and intricate pattern, and the creative reader will do likewise. Time and space sequences are incidental.

This last work coincides in time with the latter half of *New England: Indian Summer* and in space with the Melville-Whitman book. Opening with the New York of the Eighties, it uses the arrival of James Huneker in 1886 to strike its keynote in much the way Gilbert Stuart and Horace Greeley were used in earlier volumes. The first twenty-nine chapters maintain the now-familiar calmness of temper and objectivity of the chronicler. This is the time and this the world of Mr. Brooks himself; but nowhere is he mentioned. Even his closer intimates like John Hall Wheelock, Lewis Mumford, Waldo Frank, and James Oppenheim—the circle of *The Freeman* and *The Seven Arts*—are omitted or scarcely mentioned. The role he himself played in bringing the confident years to a close with the anti-Puritan and the Mark Twain (still the most seminal of his writings) and Henry James books is given to Randolph Bourne, only momentarily important and long since departed. For the rest, this is the world of Edith Wharton, of Theodore Dreiser, of Norris and Garland, of the early Lewis and O'Neill.

Those who have read the earlier books will not need to be told that the picture is both vivid and colorful, accurate in bold outlines and important details. Real people move through scenes like characters in an historical romance, and ideas have the firmness and roundness of well-drawn people. Nowhere is the author or reader confused by the confusions of mind and emotion of these changing times. This is a panorama, not a dissection, of the past, a pageant of literary America. Mr. Brooks works best when he knows and loves his material, and he knows and loves the Concord of Emerson and the New York of the recent past. Volumes II and IV are logical necessities in the over-all plan. This and the New England books are effortless and convincing.

There is criticism—usually tolerant, wise and shrewd—but it is of authors as people in an environment rather than of the things they wrote. Writers as different as Gertrude Stein and Edith Wharton receive equally sympathetic treatment because they depicted honestly the life they knew and so contributed to the unfolding of the American past, while harsh comment on H. L. Mencken and Paul Elmer More is directed toward their own rejections of the creative spirit of their times. Happily but inconclusively, this chronicle of America's literary past concludes with Eugene O'Neill, "uncertain, tentative, puzzled, and groping."

At this point Mr. Brooks drops his role of impartial observer of the crystal ball and dons that of his own Oliver Allston, the man of opinions. The last two chapters of *The Confident Years* (by the way, a title reminiscent of Henry Canby's *The Age of Confidence*) review hastily the literary climax of the Twenties and Thirties and close with a vigorous challenge to the leadership (Delmore Schwarz has called it "dictatorship") of T. S. Eliot over his generation. For Brooks was once himself a general, and old generals, it is said, never die. There is still great consistency and importance in the now unfashionable critical ideas of this battle-scarred veteran!

For the present let it be noted that the point of the quarrel is more fairly and cogently stated here than it was in the "Coterie" name-calling of the Allston book. Here the challenge is explicit: Eliot, the rediscoverer of the values of literary tradition, has rejected the American tradition, and American writers have accepted his dictum. Even Ezra Pound or Gertrude Stein or H. L. Mencken or Henry James committed no such crime as this; for each of them accepted as premise the vitality and diversity of the American genius as something worthy at least to fight with. On the other hand, Eliot, by his effort to "re-establish the ancient connection between literary tradition and the orthodoxy that America had abandoned," has almost succeeded in accomplishing what Jonathan Edwards and Paul Elmer More and other fundamentalists of varying creeds have from time to time unsuccessfully attempted, the denial of democracy. Brooks takes his stand with Jefferson, Emerson, Whitman, Wolfe, Frost, and now Faulkner in asserting that faith in human dignity and progress—the ethical core of the democratic tradition—cannot perish and must not be denied. In doing so, he has resolved his own former dichotomy, the "high-brow" idealism of "our poets" and the "low-brow" naturalism of the present century. In these last two chapters of his fifth and final volume he steps down from the historian's rostrum to make clear the critical purpose of the whole series.

"A people," this same critic wrote in 1915, "is like a ciphered parchment which has to be held up to the fire before its hidden significances come out . . . and certainly the man who can throw American life into relief will be a man out of ninety million."

28

1951

THE MODERN NOVEL IN AMERICA, 1900-1950
by Frederick J. Hoffman[1]

FIFTY YEARS OF THE AMERICAN NOVEL
edited by Harold C. Gardiner, S.J.[2]

One of the most popular approaches to the historical study of literature, as we have seen, is to divide it into "types." The four major types—fiction, poetry, drama, and essay or criticism—can be subdivided into subtypes, as fiction into novel and short story; poetry into lyric, epic, narrative, dramatic; drama into tragedy, comedy, history; and essay into literary or social criticism, nonfiction prose, or the familiar essay. Among other types are, of course, ballad, satire, farce, and journalism.

This was one of the underlying principles of organization in LHUS and the two books here under review are grouped by this rubric: they both deal with the twentieth-century novel. Mr. Hoffman's is by far the more important. A perceptive analytical critic, he was also able to maintain a sense of historical development. In this same Regnery series, Downar's history of twentieth-century drama and O'Connor's of literary

---

1. Chicago: Henry Regnery Company, 1951.

2. New York: Charles Scribner's Sons, 1951. Reviewed in *Saturday Review* 35 (February 2, 1952): 20.

criticism were almost equally successful, even though Louise Bogan's study of poetry (review 29, pp. 96-97) was more personal, selective, and nonhistorical. Less bound to its social condition than in the larger work, a poem or novel could find its historical continuity in the rise or fall of movements, styles, or fashions. A comprehensive history of all of American literature might be organized on this basic principle, and certainly the "types" approach was worth watching.

Both these books have basic judicial systems of values that somewhat distort historical perspective; both, in the final analysis, are more successful as critical studies than as literary history.

As the twentieth century moves into its third quarter, it leaves behind it a body of American literature that is worthy of comparison with almost any group of writings of any time or place. Furthermore, during these fifty years, the novel has moved up to first place among literary forms for range, depth, meaning, and technical versatility. A short history of the twentieth-century American novel invites speculation beyond the limits of its covers; two such histories invite comparison.

Mr. Hoffman's book is one of a series of six short surveys of types of twentieth-century American literature to be issued by the same publisher. As one of the two general editors of the series, he could, of course, write his own ticket, but he applies to his own book (potentially the bulkiest of them all) the same strict limitations he has imposed on the others. Compression, speed, and generalization from limited evidence mark every page, but so do clear perspective and a sense of historical progress. The hypothesis that the American novel learned from Henry James the technical control necessary to make effective Frank Norris's desire for "life" is applied to naturalistic novels from Dreiser to Faulkner and beyond. Throughout, Mr. Hoffman uses as guides the insights of his training in psychoanalysis and the New Criticism.

The second work, a compilation of sixteen essays, most of them critical appraisals of single novelists of the period, declares its purpose in the editor's first chapter, "A Christian Appraisal." Quoting

Stuart Sherman (who had a slightly different idea in mind), Father Gardiner frankly declares: "We value our critics in proportion to the soundness and the abundance of their preconceptions and in proportion to the adequacy of their ulterior purposes." In about two-thirds of the essays, these "ulterior purposes" provide firm grounds for judgment of each author and his works, although the judgment in most cases is broadly humane (catholic in the general sense) rather than doctrinaire.

Neither book is objective history; both are criticisms in historical sequence or arrangement. Although their critical premises and principles differ drastically, Father Gardiner and Mr. Hoffman agree in using a priori methods, in their choice and general arrangement of major authors, and in their attitudes toward the naturalistic movement. They tell essentially the same story but they evaluate it quite differently.

Their lists of novelists to be included are almost identical. Edith Wharton, Ellen Glasgow, Theodore Dreiser, and Willa Cather survive from the first generation; while the Bohemians, the historical romancers, and the drawing-room sentimentalists so popular in the first two decades of the century have disappeared. From the Twenties both books choose Sinclair Lewis, Scott Fitzgerald, John Dos Passos, and Ernest Hemingway. Mr. Hoffman takes time out for a careful analysis of the combined influence of Gertrude Stein and Ezra Pound while Father Gardiner includes an essay on John P. Marquand; but one may search the index unrewardingly for significant comment on Joseph Hergesheimer, Glenway Wescott, Hervey Allen, Kenneth Roberts, Vardis Fisher, and Louis Bromfield. Both books give the Thirties to Faulkner, Wolfe, Steinbeck, and Farrell (not Erskine Caldwell), praise Faulkner highly for slightly different reasons, and agree in condemning the other three for much the same reason. Both critics grant Norman Mailer first place among novelists of World War II, using this fact as evidence of a nearly complete decay of taste and value in this group of writers; and both have already forgotten Budd Schulberg and Ross Lockridge while trying to forget James Jones. Finally, both books settle for the "novel of ideas" as represented by Robert Penn Warren as the best hope for the future. Mr. Hoffman adds first honors for Lionel

Trilling's wooden *The Middle of the Journey,* while Father Gardiner's contributor points with sounder instinct to the almost forgotten (because conventional) achievement of James Gould Cozzens. A check of other critical histories of this subject would confirm the conclusion that there is by now an established pantheon even though the gods composing it are worshiped with varying degrees of reverence.

Even more striking is the agreement in these two books that naturalism is the villain in the story. If Mr. Hoffman did not reveal in his opening paragraph on Frank Norris's preference for "raw life" over "fine style," his own preference for "fine style" over "raw life," his concluding paragraph would make the point: "There is no reason to believe that the flood of naturalist novels should continue unabated in the future. . . . The opportunities for the writing of good fiction now seem even greater than they ever were before." But Mr. Hoffman is a better critic by instinct than he is by method. He often chooses the really fine book for critical discussion and then explores its "fictional strategies" rather than its meaning and value. He often spoils a good idea by use of wrist-smacking patter, and he avoids responsibility for exact critical definition by putting his terms in quotes without giving their source in this special meaning. These are bad habits of some of the lesser of contemporary critics, but good men also fall into a fashion. Fortunately, his imperfect sympathy for naturalism influences his pronouncements on individual authors without seriously dislocating his historical perspective. A model of concise thinking and writing, his book has only the faults which its author has adopted as virtues.

Father Gardiner's company of critics joins Mr. Hoffman in attacking naturalism, not because they wish fine style, but because they seek a "spiritual answer" to contemporary "moral dislocation." They are more deeply aware than is Mr. Hoffman of the value of the modern restudy of the eternal tragic issues of human destiny, and most of them are content at the last with a lingering regret that the author and his characters failed to take the easy step from the human to the spiritual level.

There is not as much difference between the two books as one might expect because they both base the critical process on sets of predetermined values. That the two sets of values here represented are wholly different is not so important a fact as is the common critical process. Both books assume that naturalism in twentieth-century fiction is a state of mind which must be overcome before the novel can achieve its full stature. Actually, there is some doubt about whether there could have been a twentieth-century novel without the impetus and direction that naturalism from Frank Norris to James Jones has given it. A code of criticism which assumes that the central driving force of a literary movement is something to be overcome should itself be looked on with a healthy skepticism.

29

1951

ACHIEVEMENT IN AMERICAN POETRY
by Louise Bogan

Little need be added about Bogan's effort to do for twentieth-century poetry what Hoffman did for the novel. Her attempt to do her part in producing a sociopsychological history of the "type" splits apart between the intuitive criticisms of a sensitive poet and the half-understood systems and methods of the professional literary historian.

This brief survey of twentieth-century poetry in America is one of six books which together attempt to review and evaluate American literature by types during the first half of the century. This book differs from some of the others in that Miss Bogan is herself a poet and critic of note rather than an academic scholar, and her book is a personal essay rather than a work of historical objectivity. It also differs in that the author devotes a substantial number of her few pages to French, Irish, Spanish, and British poets who have been influential in America at a sacrifice of careful analysis of the work of poets who have been native and resident in this country. The result is an essay on modern poetry rather than on American poetry, in which Rilke receives almost as much attention as Frost, Auden rather more than either of them, and the team of Pound and Eliot approximately as much as all other individual American poets put together. The book therefore cannot be taken seriously as a history of twentieth-century American poetry.

Chicago: Henry Regnery Company, 1951. Reviewed in *American Literature* 25 (March 1953): 117-118.

It can, however, be taken seriously as an essay written to a well-defined and rather generally accepted thesis: that T. S. Eliot discovered an aesthetic which successfully resolved the confusions of modern industrial man and made his experience once more available to poetic insight. Pound, according to this view, prepared the way for the master by his ubiquitous experimentation and protest; and Wallace Stevens, W. C. Williams, and Marianne Moore learned enough of the new way to write distinguished if not great poetry. Other poets like Frost, Sandburg, Hart Crane, and younger poets like Karl Shapiro are measured according to their relative distances from the central light. In Eliot, the new freedoms become the new discipline of interpretation. His own achievement in *The Waste Land* and *Four Quartets* adequately meets the requirements of his critical theory and provides fixed poles of reference for all lines of poetic development in the period.

This statement is something of an oversimplification of what is itself a vast oversimplification of the facts. But it is the essential gospel of an increasingly articulate group of contemporary poets and critics of poetry. In attempting to give it historical validity, Miss Bogan has indulged in many pages of generalizations about cultural facts and movements and parallel developments in other arts and in the arts of other countries. Most of these have at least some of their roots in facts, but they are offered so generously that they can be defended neither logically nor chronologically. Her method can be accepted only if her book is taken as a provocative essay by a sensitive and exciting imagination. Keen insights, stimulated rather than supported by wide and eclectic reading, have produced a book which should open its subject up to further study and perhaps to sounder historical analysis.

30

1953

REBELS AND ANCESTORS: THE AMERICAN NOVEL, 1890-1915
by Maxwell Geismar

Maxwell Geismar had meanwhile been doing book after book on the history of modern American fiction in relationship to American life and had now brought his story from the contemporary, with which he started, back to the period of Van Wyck Brooks's final volume. Future historians and critics of American literature will find in his work one of the most consistent applications of the scientifically determined approach to American literary history since Parrington, with insights derived from biological and psychological, as well as socio-economic factors.

My review called out a letter from Max, which is perhaps worth quoting in part because it hints at some of the ways we literary historians were pushing out at that time into the behavioral sciences: "That was the review I was really looking for, and I thought the books deserved," he wrote. "You did it with great insight, warmth, and generosity, and I am grateful, in the deepest way, to you. . . . What you also did was to crystalize and bring out the meaning of the series in a way I had never consciously formulated for myself. . . . I would like to discuss the psychological thing more fully sometime than we had chance to the other day. It is an issue I had to resolve while writing the book, not a trap I fell into."

Boston: Houghton Mifflin Company, 1953. Reviewed in *Saturday Review of Literature* 36 (October 3, 1953): 33.

It would almost seem that the literary critics of the present time could be divided into two main groups by the simple question of whether or not, in their view, a work of art is rooted in the society of its time. Maxwell Geismar is one of those who would give a strong affirmative answer to that question and so separate himself from at least the more extreme of the New Critics. He is primarily a critic of culture (of which literature is one expression) and his work assumes importance at a time when literary criticism seems to be leaning rather toward the analytic and more purely aesthetic methods.

Rebels and Ancestors is the third work in a series which attempts to analyze modern American fiction as an expression of modern American life. Starting with *Writers in Crisis* in 1942, Mr. Geismar stated his problem and set his method in an analysis of the work of the so-called "lost generation." With *The Last of the Provincials* he moved back to a group of writers of the "middle" period, 1915-1925, in whose work the central problems of contemporary fiction were first clearly stated; and now he carries his exploration further back to the sources of this modern movement in the writers of the period 1890-1915. Whether he has in mind a book on the first of the "realists," Howells, James, Mark Twain, and their contemporaries, he does not say, but such a book is not needed, either in general or for the purpose of his grand design. The nature of the twentieth-century revolt, despair, and fulfillment in literature has been now exposed in the terms this critic set himself. The result is one of the most ambitious contemporary attempts at cultural criticism, a pioneering work in both subject and method.

Perhaps it is not altogether fair to present Mr. Geismar's controlling thesis first when he has tried so hard to avoid dogmatism by saving his statement of principles for the last chapter of his third book. The complex of modern American life, Mr. Geismar seems to believe, may be studied on three levels: the biological, the sociological, and the psychological. On the first, the drive is toward the scientific detachment of the naturalist, and the violent primitivism of the social Darwinians; on the second, it is toward the apparent failure of the American dream and the narrow escape from a Marxian solution of the resulting despair; on the third, it is toward the release of repressed motivation, principally sexual, which gives to the most hidden of personal problems the force of social significance by an extension of the Freudian hypothesis to group behavior.

In each of his three books, Mr. Geismar limits his study to no more than six leading and representative figures; in this one his subjects are Frank Norris, Stephen Crane, Jack London, Ellen Glasgow, and Theodore Dreiser, the writers of fiction of this period who, in his estimation, most emphatically broke with the "ancestors" and most effectually prepared for the "rebels." Each one is given a full chapter of analysis, simultaneously on three levels, without too much direct reference to companion studies or to emerging generalizations.

Of the three levels of analysis, the social is by far the most effective. The ten-page essay at the end on "Theories of the Dreamers" is the real heart of Mr. Geismar's thinking. "Reading over the literature of the progressive movement in the 1900s," he concludes, "you almost have the sense of 'the submerged truth'—or a hidden body of facts which, with all its distortions, errors, and false hopes, also contained the most brilliant and fruitful source of American social criticism yet compiled."

It is that "hidden body of facts" that the three books have followed through, and in doing so, they have helped more than any other work of contemporary historical criticism to clarify a paradox in American literary history: i.e., why the great literature of a democracy must be self-critical almost to the point of self-destruction. Because our writers have consistently condemned the materialism and selfishness of the democratic capitalistic form of society, Europeans almost to a man (and many Americans) have concluded that we have produced a great literature in spite of the conditions of American life, and that under some other system (preferably some form of totalitarianism) we might have produced an even greater art. The tragedy of this misunderstanding is so great that any critic who can help to resolve it deserves a Congressional Medal, and Mr. Geismar's study does help by revealing the direct connection between the actual conditions of American life and the literature it has produced. Only in an open society can criticism of life be unrestricted in art; and only when such criticism of life is possible can the most searching and meaningful art result.

In the essay on Dreiser, the social problem is most successfully illuminated by reference to the personal and natural levels of analysis. It is perhaps the best short essay on this Titan; and that on Ellen Glasgow is not far below it in excellence. In that on London, where the biological is predominant, the analysis is steady but not quite as well focused. Partly because the Freudian hypothesis as a general and literary influence does not belong historically to the period here under study, and partly because Mr. Geismar is less sure and more doctrinaire in its application than he is with social systems, the chapters on Crane and Norris snag badly on Oedipean and castration theories. Influenced too much by John Berryman's pseudo-Freudian diagnosis of Crane in a recent and misleading biography, the social critic temporarily loses his perspective as these two authors slip from his grasp.

Social psychology, if it is to play its important part in cultural study, must avoid the easy, the trite, the doctrinaire solution that would fix all human motivation on a classic character named Oedipus. It is interesting that Mr. Geismar did not make use of the full documentation of his fears of impotence provided by Dreiser in his autobiographical *Dawn,* but in that case keeps the psychological motivation in firm relationship with the social. In such moments he asserts his right to high place as a literary critic.

31

1958

❦AMERICAN LITERATURE ❧
AND CHRISTIAN DOCTRINE
by Randall Stewart

As the basic thesis that literature is the aesthetic expression of the culture in which it occurs took root, scholars began to turn from a study of literary history as such to that of the culture itself. Together with the economic doctrine of a Marx, the psychological doctrine of a Freud, the democratic doctrine of a Jefferson, and the transcendentalism of an Emerson, the fundamentalist doctrine of the orthodox Christian church took its place in this book as one of the principal intellectual branches of the American tradition. It had always been assumed that ''Puritanism'' was the basic faith of at least the New England settlers, but the definition of the term did not always limit it to hard-core orthodoxy. Randall Stewart's challenge helped to clear the issue: the South too had its fundamentalist doctrine.

A linking of the liberal tradition in religion with the democratic tradition in politics has been so much a part of our cultural history for so long that a challenge to it is almost shocking. The idea that man is basically good and is infinitely capable of self-improvement seems to some a necessary premise to the idea that all men share the ''unalienable Rights'' of ''Life, Liberty and the Pursuit of Happiness.'' Inevitably, the contrary doctrine that man is born in sin

Baton Rouge: Louisiana State University Press, 1958. Reviewed in *New York Times Book Review,* June 1, 1958: p. 6.

and can be redeemed only through grace has seemed un-American and undemocratic.

Randall Stewart's argument in this brief, readable and highly persuasive tract is that the assumptions of orthodox Christian doctrine, as formulated by the New England Puritans and carried forward by the conservative wings of both the Evangelical and the Catholic churches, is perhaps more American and certainly no less democratic a religious tradition, and that it has its own hierarchy of authors from Jonathan Edwards through Hawthorne and Melville and Henry James to Eliot and Faulkner today.

A part of the current reaction against "progressivism" in all its forms, this point needed to be made because it is incontestably valid and because it has been neglected. "Puritanism" fell afoul of the radical thinking of the Twenties and Thirties; now it has its time for reinstatement. Without the orthodox formulation of the story of man and the divine tragedy of the eternal war between good and evil, much of the cultural heritage of Western Europe would be meaningless. There is no doubt that our historians have neglected or misinterpreted the part played in our literature by this body of doctrine because of lack of sympathy with it as a formulation of Christian faith.

Mr. Stewart offers a needed correction. He writes:

"If the question were looked into properly, it might be discovered that orthodox Christian doctrine offers the best rationale for democracy of all rationales. . . . I refer to St. Paul's text, 'All have sinned, and come short of the glory of God.'"

Yet in spite of its humility of tone this book commits an error as serious as that which it set out to correct. In defending the code formulated by Christian thinkers from St. Paul to Calvin and which even survived and was strengthened by the Reformation as the only true Christian doctrine, Mr. Stewart tells only half the story. The liberal tradition which is derived from a direct reading of the living Christ of the Gospels and which has survived in a persistent and consistent series of "heresies" is surely Christian also and is equally a part of the cultural heritage of Western European and American man.

To dismiss the Antinomians, the Unitarians, the transcendentalists and others of their kind as non-Christian or partially Christian is to think in terms of narrow doctrine rather than historical perspective. Edwards and Jefferson are equally our intellectual fathers, and Melville and Whitman are equally legitimate as their Christian and democratic sons. Emerson's dualistic acceptance of both Unity and Necessity in his essay on "Fate" and Hawthorne's humanitarian sympathy for the fallen Hester (which is far more than mere "compassion") suggest that the American Christian tragedy is enriched by its very ambiguities. Mr. Stewart, Professor of English at Vanderbilt and author of a life of Hawthorne, hopes that there will be other books on this subject. His hope is likely to be fulfilled.

32

1960

AMERICAN WRITING IN THE TWENTIETH CENTURY
by Willard Thorp

It is fitting that I should conclude this collection of my reviews of works in American literary history with a book by Willard Thorp, the backbone of the editorial board of the *Literary History of the United States,* at a time when we were beginning to prepare that work for its third and really definitive edition.

Thorp's interests and abilities were on every point in harmony with, but supplementary to, mine. Whereas I was most concerned with the philosophy and structure of the whole, he was interested in the specific problem, the specific chapter, the specific author, the perfection of detail. He could have written any chapter in the book, but he left the organizing of the overall history primarily to me. He was the most informed and perceptive of us all in designing special chapters and in suggesting contributors, and his study of twentieth-century literature reflects these special gifts. It is a series of critical essays on aspects of the subject, forged in urbane wisdom and written with the simplicity and lucid style that illuminates as it conceals deep learning. This is a pioneering and still one of the best books about its subject, but it is a collection of related studies in historical criticism rather than a chapter in literary history.

Cambridge: Harvard University Press, 1960. Reviewed in *New York Times Book Review,* May 29, 1960, p. 4.

By now it is pretty well agreed that the United States experienced during the past half century one of its two greatest literary periods —perhaps its greatest period. The writings of O'Neill, Hemingway, Frost, Faulkner, Eliot and some others are recognized throughout the world as masterpieces of contemporary art. Yet American critics and historians have persistently missed the reasons for our pre-eminence and have apologized for the pessimism or realism or critical "anti-Americanism" of these same writers. How, they ask, can a writer be good if he doesn't believe in God and praise the American way of life? Our literature should carry the faith of Jefferson to the Hottentots or it is not worthy of us.

Willard Thorp, chairman of the Department of English at Princeton, resolves this paradox by ignoring it. He merely tells his story as he knows it and sees it. The result is a book of quiet mastery and convincing authority, the first really definitive treatment of our modern literary achievement. A series of essays in historical criticism rather than a systematic literary history, it nevertheless manages to cover the four main literary genres—fiction (two chapters), poetry (also two), and drama and literary criticism (one each). There are bonus chapters on the decline of the genteel tradition and on the renaissance merely because these subjects are important. The method within each chapter is mainly chronological, and repetitions are cross-keyed in footnotes, but there is only a vague chronological movement through the book as a whole. Each essay has its own central theme, and each concludes with a brief critical appraisal of a major author, but otherwise the only continuity from chapter to chapter lies in the subject itself and in Mr. Thorp's own sane and comprehensive grasp of it in its entirety.

Right there is the secret of the sense of mastery that the book conveys. Here at last is a critic who can explain to us why naturalism, with all its sordid details and its usually fatalistic philosophy, has produced and is still producing some of our most powerful novels, and at the same time he can explain why the new criticism has given our poetry discipline, form, technical mastery and intellectual integrity. He can trace the effect of Marxism in our writing during the Thirties and of Freudianism today without becoming a partisan or an anti-Communist or Freudian. He can let himself go in his obvious love of the South without forgetting the brief Chicago "renaissance" or the literary importance of New England and California. He can be pure literary critic without losing his social and historical bearings.

Such scholarship is always deceptive because its hard-earned insights and conclusions are likely to seem the simple truths that we have known all the while, once they are stated in the lucid prose of which Mr. Thorp is so fine a master. But let it be here said: This is the book to give the Hottentots who want to know why American literature today is so strong that it need not shrink from dealing honestly with the worst as well as the best in human nature. Until someone does better—and that should be a long while—this is the authority on twentieth-century American literature. Like the literature that it writes about, it is the firm voice of a mature and free people.

Epilogue

1973

✠ HISTORY OF A HISTORY ✠

The Story Behind
Literary History of the United States

Although an aura of anonymity seemed appropriate when LHUS first appeared, the publication of a revised fourth edition in 1974 made it less necessary. The story behind the story could now be told, and I was surprised to find how inaccurate my memory was when I consulted the archives in the University of Pennsylvania Library. The following account was published in the "Professional Notes and Comments" columns of *Publications of the Modern Language Association.*

I

When *Literary History of the United States* (LHUS) appeared in November 1948, there was some confusion about how such a work came into being, and just who was responsible. The title page contained the names of Spiller, Thorp, Johnson, and Canby, with Jones, Williams, and Wecter as Associates, and a list of fifty-five leading scholars in American literature and history (including these seven) as contributors; but there was no central sponsorship other than the publisher. The chapters were unsigned and only the most determined of its readers turned to the "Table of Authors" at the end to solve the mystery of authorship. The 817-page *Bibliography* volume was equally anonymous, even though it was a separate but supporting work with a mind of its own. No wonder the scholars and journalists who reviewed it, the librarians, and the public, after a valiant struggle with the problem, gave up in confusion and created a mythical author-editor, "Spiller et. al." So I became, like the Spencer Brydon of Henry James, a man haunted by himself; and now, when I meet new people—often those who owe their Ph.D.'s to good cramming sessions with this book—their faces momentarily expose their surprise that I am a real human being and not merely a name on the library shelf. But there seems to be no doubt in their minds that the book itself is very much alive as the major work in its field throughout the world.

The first reception of LHUS in 1948 was a bit uneven. "Here is God's plenty," announced one reviewer; "a literary shambles," commented another; "a basic document for our age," wrote Perry Miller in the *New York Times,* but "covered with academic mold," countered Lewis Gannett in the *Herald Tribune.* But perhaps the most perceptive comment was Norman Pearson's in the *Saturday Review of Literature:* "The basis of the book is one of historical perspective and balance. Its triumphs are editorial." That was the real goal our little editorial board of four set for itself back in August 1942, when we met for the first time for a full two-day conference at Henry Canby's cottage at Yelping Hill, West Cornwall, Connecticut. Our task was to weld fifty-five (as it turned out) diverse creative minds into a single committed mind and then to produce a flowing narrative and critical account of the making and shaping of the whole literature of the American people in its evolving cultural context.

"Each generation," we believed, "must define the past in its own terms," and we hoped to create a situation in which our generation could speak by committing ourselves and by agreeing at the start on a rigorously disciplined organization in which each of us had his individual role and responsibility, a carefully developed plan and outline in which all values and procedures were thought through and defined, and a covering mantle of semi-anonymity to which both editors and contributors were asked to agree. The book then wrote itself.

The history of this history is so complicated that I had determined until recently to let someone else unravel it from the complete archives at the University of Pennsylvania Library, and from the minutes of the American Literature Group (then a subdivision of the Modern Language Association) which are at the University of Wisconsin in Madison. However, it now seems to me that my interpretation of these documents might be useful, if not taken as the final word.

As the history of the project unfolded, it became clear to me that our experience might not be unique. We had set out, in our early discussions, to produce cooperatively an official Group project, a broadly conceived and carefully documented interpretation of the history of American literature; but soon the project began to build up an opposition by the mere fact of its success. People who had been nourishing similar plans for years felt challenged and regional loyalties were awakened. How the project was finally stalled within the Group and subsequently became a private enterprise is becoming more clear, but as to just who was involved and what the nature of the countermovement actually was I am still unsure. Unfortunately, the experience is all too common in cooperative scholarly projects. Who is at fault when such things happen, and what can be done about it? Such questions do not lend themselves to a single answer, but in going back to the archives of LHUS after twenty-five years, I have discovered many things and many explanations of things I was unaware of at the time that make that first Yelping Hill weekend when the book finally began to take shape seem more like the course of destiny than the accidental whim of a group of ambitious young scholars.

II

Perhaps the best place to start is with an entry in the minutes of the Ann Arbor meeting of the infant American Literature Group of the Modern Language Association in 1923 which "favored presenting American literature as expression of national (historical) consciousness and not as aesthetic offshoot of English literature." Fred Lewis Pattee's paper, read on that occasion, became in 1924 the basis of his "Call for a Literary Historian," in the June *American Mercury* and was used as a launching pad for the unofficial Group volume of 1928, *The Reinterpretation of American Litera-*

ture, edited by Norman Foerster. Meanwhile, the first two volumes of V. L. Parrington's *Main Currents in American Thought* had appeared in 1927, and the foundations for the movement toward a new history of American literature had been laid. That this was only a decade after the first volume of the compendious *Cambridge History of American Literature* had appeared would indicate that, from the start, scholars in the new discipline felt the need for interpretation as well as accumulation of facts. The CHAL never pretended to be anything but a collection of essays on every variety of American writing arranged roughly by chronology on the subject; the plan for LHUS, on the other hand, was preceded by thorough philosophical discussions of the nature of literary history in itself and of the peculiar conditions of its growth that make American literary history indigenous and unique.

LHUS shared, of course, in the impulse of radical nationalism, social ferment, and reassessment of the native tradition that has followed every successful American war—the Revolution, the Civil War, and the two World Wars—and in the argument that political independence and world power should be followed by cultural independence and a position as one of the world literatures. However falacious, this argument provides an impelling incentive to self-respect and self-evaluation. The movement toward cultural nationalism that began in the twenties of this century had achieved worldwide acknowledgment by the forties and undeniably influenced the LHUS editors to answer an insistent call for a new literary history at that time.

But beyond and beneath this obvious motivation, the project was pushed into being by the force of two arguments derived from the traditions of European historiography and developed respectively by V. L. Parrington and Norman Foerster in 1927-28. The Parrington thesis is too well known, both for its validity and for its defects, to need much elaboration here. Formulated by Karl Marx in its earlier form, but applied by Parrington to Jeffersonian democratic and agrarian theory, it was based primarily on economic and political theory, the industrial revolution and laissez-faire, of nineteenth-tural history were "English independency, French romantic political theory, the industrial revolution and laissez-faire, of nineteenth century science, and of Continental theories of collectivism."

Parrington frankly admits that he chose to follow "the broad path of our political, economic, and social development" and that "the main divisions of the study have been fixed by forces that are anterior to literary schools and movements, creating the body of ideas from which literary culture eventually springs."[1] The weakness of this position as a basic theory of literary historiography is that it deliberately avoids the problem of critical evaluation of literature as an art; its usefulness to the literary historian of its day was that it cut the linguistic umbilical cord that had bound American literary theory to the literary tradition of Great Britain alone, excluding both its own and general European and Oriental sources. The dominance of the English language in America tends to distort the cosmopolitan nature of the culture.

The contribution of Norman Foerster was even more important to the LHUS editors than that of Parrington, but it has been largely forgotten. In his Preface to the *Reinterpretation* volume, Foerster succinctly states his case:

> We are increasingly aware of the inadequacy of the traditional estimates formulated in the last century, the century in which the bulk of our literature was written. . . . To the problems of criticism the American scholar cannot afford to be indifferent, and for two reasons: the first because . . . he is compelled to decide what literature deserves attention on critical grounds; and secondly because, in his capacity as literary historian, he cannot fulfill the whole of his task unless he seeks to account for the success of literary works in so far as this success is the result of their aesthetic qualities. The historical scholar attains his most striking triumphs when dealing with inferior literature. . . . Although brief success may be accounted for by temporary and nonaesthetic causes, protracted success issues from excellences that are largely timeless and aesthetic, and permanent success from excellences that are wholly so. . . . A thoroughgoing historian must also be a critic.[2]

In his chapter on "Factors in American Literary History" which follows, Foerster applies his thesis to the immediate problem of the distinctiveness of American literary history. "All factors may be comprised under two heads: European culture and American environment. American history, including literary history, is to be viewed as the interplay of these two tremendous factors, neither of which has been studied profoundly by our literary scholars. Because they are tremendous, however, they must be divided into a serviceable number of lesser factors, and from such a list (which I must leave hypothetical) I will select the four that seem to me most important. They are (1) the Puritan tradition, (2) the frontier spirit, (3) romanticism, and (4) realism'' (p. 26).

The first and second of these factors are conditioning and preparatory factors; the third and fourth describe the two periods of literary achievement that developed out of but also rose far above the conditioning factors to which Parrington limited himself, and prove Foerster to be a historical critic rather than merely a literary historian.

How these two theories helped, each in its own way, to shape LHUS is revealed in the first memorandum of the editors to the contributors:

> Literary history is defined as the description and evaluation of those writings which for their intrinsic merit as expressions of experience, are worthy of preservation. It is history in that such writings are arranged and accounted for in their historical contexts. It is "American" in that the experience recounted must have its roots within what is now the United States. The planning of the book, therefore, has proceeded from discussions of the writings of major authors, to those of minor authors, to those of intellectual, social, and circumstantial factors in so far as they determined the form and content of these writings. Chronology as such is subordinate.
>
> The outline reverses this procedure, furnishing chapters on the intellectual, social, and circumstantial factors first, usually chapters dealing with groups of minor authors next, and finally separate chapters on major authors. . . . The work as a whole reaches two climactic points: that of the mid-nineteenth-century major authors, and that of the literature of the present.

Much of this rationale is buried in the vast mass of data subsumed by the final work, although it is clearly outlined in the division by "Books" and "Chapters" in the table of contents. For this reason, I later wrote a condensation, while the larger view was still fresh in my mind, which even tended to overstress the ideological frame and critical principles that had guided us. This was *The Cycle of American*

Literature.[3] For this book, and for the so-called "cycle" theory which was derived from it, I alone take responsibility, even though that theory in its final form was not entirely original with me. I proposed it in outline in an early essay,[4] but its final form grew out of our group discussions and became the core of our thinking for the big book.

III

There was an interval of a decade between the formulation of this theoretical base for a new American literary history and the launching of the project in 1938 by the American Literature Group of the Modern Language Association. Although I was Group Chairman in 1930 and 1931, I first came actively into the history project with a paper on "The Task of the Historian of American Literature"[5] which I read to the Group in 1935, and in which I basically accepted the Foerster formulation but called for patience while much spade-work was done to fill it out.

At a meeting of the Advisory Council of the Group at Columbia University in 1938, I stepped out for a half-hour to keep an appointment, only to learn on my return that Henry Canby had moved for the setting up of a committee on a cooperative literary history, with Bradley of Pennsylvania, Canby of Yale and New York City, Rusk of Columbia, Williams of Yale, and T. K. Whipple, then on leave from California, as members, and myself as Chairman. Proximity to each other and to the publishing center of New York City allowed us to meet frequently during that year, and, by December 1939, we had a full and detailed report, including several publishing possibilities, to present at the MLA Annual Convention in New Orleans. The Committee then proposed a ten-volume work, composed of a series of monographs by many individuals, with a supplementary survey in one to three volumes based on the larger work but designed "for the general as well as the scholarly public," and a comprehensive bibliography, also in one to three volumes.

In spite of a small attendance and probably in part because of the support of the Chairman, Jay B. Hubbell of Duke, and the Secretary, Tremaine McDowell of Minnesota, the report was enthusiastically accepted and the Committee was given "power to sign a contract and arrange the mechanical details of publication and to provide machinery for selecting a permanent editorial board, which shall determine the approach and methods to be employed."[6] One major incentive to this spirit of optimism was a letter from George P. Brett, Jr., President of the Macmillan Company. Macmillan was prepared to sign a contract for the multivolumed history, with a $10,000 advance against royalties and an additional $10,000 in outright subsidy. From that moment, George Brett stood firmly behind me in all my endeavors.

It is clear now, however, that the enthusiasm of success had caused both the Committee and the Group to overlook evidences of an emerging opposition. In October 1939, two months before the New Orleans meeting, Napier Wilt, the nominee for the next year's Group Chairman, had written to me:

> Because of the project for a history of American literature, I think it would be a pretty good idea to devote almost all of the meeting [of 1940] to problems relating to the historiography of American literature. . . To this end I suggested that you, or some member of your committee, write an elaborate account of your plans, that this account be published in the November 1940 issue of *American Literature,* and that the papers at the meeting consist of one formal and a number of informal discussions of this plan. . . . I would much prefer not to have your paper read at the meeting but to have it in the hands of our group before the meeting so that the members can be prepared to discuss it intelligently. I rather expect the plan, whatever it is, will come in for quite a bit of criticism, and I suggest that one member of your committee be formally appointed to defend the plan.[7]

The immediate result of this warning was that the Committee agreed not to move forward in spite of the powers granted to it, but to prepare the detailed report that was asked for. The Committee felt it had something to offer but nothing to defend. Besides, by action of the Council, now under Wilt's chairmanship, its membership was increased from six to ten in order to make it more regionally representative. New England was represented by Howard Mumford Jones of Harvard, the South by Jay B. Hubbell of Duke, and the Far West by Louis B. Wright, then of the Huntington Library in California (T. K. Whipple died in 1939); and Napier Wilt of the University of Chicago, as an ex officio member, represented the Middle West.

The enlargement of the Committee made it necessary to review all plans and decisions, but its wide regional distribution made meetings in person impossible due to lack of travel funds. All business during this year was therefore conducted by correspondence, but by fall the Committee had succeeded in preparing a comprehensive plan of action which was mailed out to the Group membership in October, together with an eleven-page essay on "Literary History and Cooperative Scholarship" by the Chairman. The report proper found the project sound from the literary, academic, and financial points of view and proposed as the next step a conference, probably to be subsidized by the American Council of Learned Societies, to initiate the editorial organization, develop an outline, fund necessary research, and arrange for publication; but it also cautioned against haste in so ambitious a project. The Chairman's essay proposed many theoretical and practical ideas which later became influential in planning the future LHUS, but stressed the desirability of aiming at comprehensive coverage in a multivolumed cooperative work, to be supplemented by an interpretive survey by one or a few authors based upon it.

For reasons I am unable to recall, neither this report nor the supplementary essay was published in the November *American Literature*—although they may have been circulated to the membership in mimeographed form—but papers by Louis Wright, Yvor Winters, and Harry Hayden Clark were. Wright called for many years of specialized research before a synthesis of any kind would be justified; Winters warned of the dangers of unenlightened specialization; and Clark advanced a theory by which the "literature of knowledge" could receive a different treatment from that accorded to the "literature of power" (De Quincey's terms).

When the Group assembled in Cambridge, Massachusetts, in late December, the Committee had little difficulty in reading the handwriting on the wall. It was not necessary to know precisely what had happened to realize that the forward thrust of the project had built up its own resistance and that the Committee's report would at best be tabled. Chairman Wilt had correctly predicted that "the plan, whatever it is, will come in for quite a bit of criticism.'' After a hasty conference in a nearby restaurant, the Committee agreed to accept the inevitable and empowered its Chairman to withdraw its proposal and to move instead for a new Committee to explore the resources in American libraries and collections. This would clear the way for the research preliminary to an ultimate synthesis. This motion avoided an open presentation of a detailed plan of action, with the resulting stigma of a probably official rejection of the whole project. After presenting this substitute motion, the Committee withdrew while the Council passed it without major changes. It then appointed a new Committee of five with widespread regional representation, and, for his sins, the same Chairman. The new Committee immediately set to work on its new assignment.

That was the end of a Group project for a new literary history of the United States.

IV

But the forces of reaction had underestimated the buoyancy and persistency of that happy warrior Henry Canby. Canby, as Editor of *Saturday Review of Literature,* had published in August 1939 (the sequence of dates here is interesting; this was two months before the original Wilt letter) an editorial entitled ''Wanted—a History,'' and he was not to be countermaneuvered. His proposal had been the emergence of another but wiser Parrington to head a small committee ''empowered to draft the research of American scholars, digest and assimilate it for a work of several volumes for that portion of the American public aware of history and craving it,'' and so provide a standard interpretive history of American literature as the subject was then understood. His own *Classic Americans* (1931) was described in the Preface as ''originally planned as a history of American literature studied in the light of its social and intellectual backgrounds,'' but ''a busy editorial life'' had forced abandonment of the plan after a preliminary essay on ''The Colonial Background'' and the completion of essays on eight major nineteenth-century writers. It was the old problem of which comes first, the cart or the horse, the material or the rationale, and I was squarely in the middle.

A week after the Cambridge meeting, Henry was in my study in Swarthmore to celebrate a private post-mortem and to invite me to join Howard Mumford Jones, Stanley Williams, and himself for a house party at his home in Killingworth, Connecticut, that spring. At the time I did not see how I could honestly serve two masters: the Group in its research project and a private team writing an interpretive synthesis; but, of course, the original proposal of my Committee had divided the project along much these lines. Was it a problem of principle, or one of means?

By 9 February, I thought I saw my way clear and wrote Henry:

Since talking with you I have been thinking pretty steadily about this proposed survey history of American literature. During our conversations I was not clear because I was still thinking in terms of some sort of definitive work and I could not quite see the justification for undertaking it while working on the long-term project. The only reason for proposing a survey now would be the conviction that we had something to say and that this is the time it should be said. The "something to say" has been growing more clear to me. . . .

The central purpose of our history might therefore be an attempt to define the spirit of the American people as expressed in our literature and traced through the steady growth of a national consciousness. This would be done by singling out the major writers and giving them full critical treatment against the background of the literary and intellectual and social movements which conditioned their development and above which they rose. We should not be lost in the morass of minor writers and of writing which is not literature. (LHUS archives)

The party at Killingworth was a great success. The spring country air, accompanied by the best of food and drink and the gracious hospitality of the lovely Lady Canby, made decisions easy and comfortable. It was unanimously agreed that such a history as Henry proposed was an urgent necessity for the sustaining of American cultural life, but that no one of the four of us had the time, energy, and sense of commitment to undertake the primary responsibility for initiating it. We adjourned planning to reconvene on Cape Cod the following summer, but for one reason or another that meeting never came off. And there the matter rested.

That is, until later that autumn when my conscience (or whatever you want to call it) caught up with me and I went back to Henry with the proposal that I undertake a somewhat different sort of work, more along the lines of the original American Literature Group project, with multiple authorship, but on a smaller scale and with my own team. Could the interpretive synthesis be done by focusing the essences of individual insight on a single structure? Vision and tact were needed.

Henry approved, George Brett renewed the Macmillan offer of a $10,000 advance against royalties for the new project, and I went to the MLA Annual Convention in Indianapolis that December to participate in a series of six round-table discussions which Chairman Wilt (in his second term) had arranged on the resources for research. But more important was an encounter at the hotel with Willard Thorp. I told him my plan and asked him to join me as editor of the text, with final responsibility for inclusiveness and accuracy. He agreed, and over lunch at the Nassau Club in Princeton on 2 June 1942, we laid out the essential guidelines for the new and now living project. I will resist the impulse to transcribe the minutes I took of this pleasant occasion. Perhaps the most important item was a decision to take the bus (this was wartime) down to nearby Lawrenceville and ask Tom Johnson to be our bibliographer. After a half-hour talk in his home, he said, "I have never before made so important a decision so quickly, but I agree."

The only remaining link in the chain to be repaired was to ask Henry Canby to join us in an active role. He reluctantly consented; in a sense, it had always been Henry's book. Howard Mumford Jones, Stanley T. Williams, and Dixon Wecter accepted posts as Associates, with advisory duties only. And so we were off to a new start.

Six years later LHUS appeared.

V

The contrast between the Cambridge meeting of the Modern Language Association and that first intimate conference of the new Editorial Board at Henry Canby's cottage at Yelping Hill a year and a half later was something of a miracle. In looking back, I am

convinced that the four survivors realized that we had each committed the best years of our professional lives, not only to the undertaking we deeply believed in, but to each other. The result was a
friendship that has lasted through all the remaining years of our
lives and has survived all changes of time and place and all conflicts
of interest. Henry Canby died some years ago and we have added
two somewhat younger editors to the Board, but the fourth edition,
published in May 1974, is the result of a single composite mind,
working along the guidelines laid down by commitment and understanding thirty years ago.

Those guidelines were worked out in a series of two-day conferences held about once a month during 1942 and 1943 in Princeton, Swarthmore, New York, and New Haven, and somewhat less
frequently during the following years. The minutes of those meetings tell the story of the slow development of a working philosophy
of literary history in the form of a synoptic outline, the careful selection of contributors who could meet the requirements of this
particular book as well as of their specializations, and the perfecting
of a legal and business agreement by which all editors and contributors were bound. I cannot spell out all these agreements in detail,
but a few of them might be of interest because they were so unusual
and so effective in protecting us from some of the hazards to which
a project of this kind is normally exposed.

In a legal contract of partnership, signed 2 January 1943 and
canceled in December 1948 after the book appeared, it was specified
that the names of the editors would always appear in a fixed order
but without discriminating titles. The book was presented as the
product of a single Board with a single mind. Behind the title page,
however, the powers and responsibilities of individual members
were clearly broken down into a Chairman, with primary responsibility for general policy, planning, and final editing, a Vice-Chairman, with primary responsibility for the text, a Secretary-Treasurer,
with primary responsibility for the bibliography, and one member
at large. Although elected for one year at a time, these four—Spiller,
Thorp, Johnson, and Canby—kept the same roles until well after
the book appeared, and there have been only essential changes since.

The Board also realized fully the weight of financial responsibility it had undertaken, and immediately set to work to find subsidy for the expenses of compilation and the payment to contribu-

tors. The first efforts in this direction bore little fruit except for a grant of $1,000 from the American Council of Learned Societies to hold conferences of editors and contributors. Two such conferences were held, at the Harvard and Columbia Clubs in New York, where contributors had a chance to compare notes and help each other integrate plans for their related chapters. In one rather amusing discussion, A. P. Hudson and Harold Thompson were convinced that we had made a mistake in assigning them the chapters on folklore and humor respectively. But we had deliberately reversed their specialties in order to get fresh thinking. After a private dinner together, they agreed to accept the assignments as we had made them. And we saw very little of Jim Farrell because that was the day the New York Vice Squad was going the rounds of the bookstores confiscating copies of *Studs Lonigan.*

The financial situation continued to look gloomy until George Brett added up his year's profits from *Gone with the Wind* and decided that some of them could be channeled into our coffers, and the Rockefeller Foundation finally granted fellowships to Spiller, Thorp, and Johnson. With this help, the editors could pay off all obligations in advance of publication and appear in the black. But during the six years of preparation, the entire group—editors, associates, and contributors—had only provisional contracts to produce a work of scholarship with uncertain rewards.

Perhaps the most unusual and effective of our guidelines was the provision that "All decisions in connection with the work of the Editorial Board shall be by unanimous vote of the Editors, except that in any case where a unanimous vote is found to be impossible, the Chairman, or the Vice-Chairman in his unavoidable absence, may make a ruling which will be binding on the other Editors." I may add that neither Thorp nor I ever had occasion to exercise these extraordinary powers, but their existence may have encouraged our unanimity. A second provision was that manuscripts would be contracted for on a fixed word count and paid for on this basis by the word, but that the Board could use its judgment in allowing latitude in actual word count as the material demanded. This allowed absolute control over both budget and bulk and undoubtedly kept the book in balance both intellectually and financially.

The development of the outline and the selection of contributors were equally well considered and painstaking. The processes required the better part of a year of meetings. No contributors were invited until the editors had worked through at least a half-dozen revisions of the outline and had developed précis and author lists for each chapter. Coverage only, and not opinions or conclusions, were specified. There were very few rejections of these invitations without sufficient cause, and very few added or altered chapters after the final outline had been adopted.

Some of the more interesting guidelines at this point were:

The book was to be written to neither a professional nor a popular audience. The readership we visualized was "a National public of intelligent lawyers, scientists, journalists, etc. as well as specialists in the literary field." This provision demanded the supplying of information beyond the requirements of the specialist and a writing style of fluidity and quality. It also explains the seemingly arbitrary occasional choice of a nonspecialist of proven scholarly and literary skill over the acknowledged authority on a given subject. For example, we learned through one of his graduate students that Matthiessen had wished to include Poe in his *American Renaissance* but found later that he did not fit into the scheme of the book. Because Poe at that time seemed to need the kind of fresh perspective that we thought Matthiessen might supply, we chose him in preference to the more thoroughly informed Quinn or Mabbott.

All manuscripts were read and criticized by the editors and associates (seven in all), but the contributor never saw the individual criticisms. He was sent a lengthy digest and advice written by the Chairman of the Board, in which differences in comments were reconciled and the author was given a single directive as to revision. When the revised manuscript came back, it was again circulated, this time only to the editors, and usually sent back for further revision. I could fill many pages by quoting some of the more spicy editorial comments on the manuscripts of the chapters as they began to come in and parts of the resulting correspondence, all of which are preserved in the LHUS archives, but let me quote just one comment by one of the Associates. After his usually scathing analysis, he was likely to conclude with the remark, "There is a difference between having to write a chapter and having a chapter to write."

The bibliography also went through several stages before it took final form and became a separate volume. At first, authors were asked to provide bibliographies for their chapters and it was planned that these lists would form the basis of a lengthy appendix to the work, arranged like the CHAL, by chapters; but it broke with that pattern when Johnson proposed that it would be more useful if designed according to its own pattern of organization. Still maintaining the principle of selectivity, it then began to develop into the original and definitive work that it became, with two major supplements edited by Richard Ludwig bringing it up to date, to the delight of all reference librarians worldwide.

But the final stage was the most radical, as described in our agreement: "The editors, in their task of unifying the material as a whole, may rewrite, or revise, or rearrange it, delete or lift matter for incorporation elsewhere, and establish the form and extent of notes and references. Manuscripts will then be returned to the contributors for approval. If a contributor, after full discussion, objects to the changes, he may refuse publication and still receive half the minimum fee . . . but nothing further."

I spent the entire summer of 1945 weaving and shaping the finished manuscript into a single book. At the least, I usually altered or supplied opening and closing sentences, or even paragraphs, for each chapter, moved sections from one chapter to another, and even restyled to the point, in a few cases, of almost rewriting. Most of the contributors accepted these revisions with only mild whimpers at the worst. My favorite example is George Whicher's comment, "Why further gild a lily that has already been gelded?" There were only a few cases in which emergency remedies were applied, and there was no case of a chapter forbidden publication by its author.

The most extreme case of compromise was that of James T. Farrell's chapter on Dreiser. It was preceded by a long correspondence on the definition of "Naturalism." Farrell explained that he had often been called a "naturalist" and he would like to understand what the term implied before he applied it to Dreiser. But when the chapter came in, it was written in the typical Farrell style, it was double the agreed length, and it avoided all historical framing. It said many good things about Dreiser, however, so I supplied a minimum of historical context and definition and cut the text stylistically in half. Quite understandably, Farrell reacted by disowning the chapter, but I could not claim the authorship because all the basic ideas and developments were his. He finally consented to publish his version in the *Chicago Review* and we published mine as "by Robert E. Spiller (based, with permission, on an article by James T. Farrell)." We split the fee and still remain friends (the University of Pennsylvania Library has all the Farrell papers). And the Dreiser chapter, although perhaps not the best thing on the subject, is integral to the rest of the book and was definitive for its time.

The other case was the much admired chapter on Henry James by R. P. Blackmur. Here I think the enforced collaboration between an analytic critic with a highly involved and characteristic style of his own and a literary historian, who, as editor, was striving for harmony and continuity in the book as a whole, was more successful. Our readers seem to agree that this is one of the most comprehensible of Blackmur's writings and one of the best of the chapters on major authors in the book. I hate to admit, therefore, that its final acceptance by the author was the result of his digging a well on his saltwater farm in Maine and going far deeper than his bank account would allow before he struck water. I quote from his letter:

> I really think that short of doing a wholly new job for you I have about exhausted my talents for revision with what I now send you. I do hope very much that it will seem suitable to you for printing much as it stands. But I hereby extend to you permission to clarify phrases and sentences, and to transpose sentences or clauses in sentences where in your opinion the presentation will benefit. . . . Lastly, will you please let me know whether you think you can use the chapter. I ask for the usual financial reasons that compel writers and professors to ask such questions. . . . If you can use the chapter, will you please send the check to me as soon as possible, and let me know that you are doing so; if you can't use it, please let me know that, too.

You may be sure I wrote him that we could use it. And we could all use more writers of Dick Blackmur's genius, humility, and integrity. His reply was characteristic.

> I am very glad since I undertook the job, it finally turned out that you could use it, and I hope that you will not have too much trouble making the details click and the connections merge properly with the remainder of the book. . . . And many, many thanks for the check

which pays for the fine cold water we have been using this past six
weeks and hope to use these fifty years to come. We got five finger-
sized holes in a ledge twenty feet down, and in this dryest (locally) of
all years, have not had less than four feet of water in the bottom.
Such are the uses of Henry James and the history of literature.

Faithfully, Dick.

NOTES

1. Vernon Louis Parrington, *The Colonial Mind,* 1620-1800, Vol. I of
Main Currents in American Thought (New York: Harcourt, 1927), p. iii.

2. *The Reinterpretation of American Literature, Some Contributions
toward the Understanding of Its Historical Development* (New York:
Harcourt, 1928), p. xiii.

3. Rev. ed. (New York: Macmillan, 1967).

4. "Blueprint for American Literary History," in my *The Third Dimension* (New York: Macmillan, 1965), pp. 26-36.

5. In *The Third Dimension,* pp. 15-25. See also "The Province of Literary
History," pp. 222-40, the mature statement of my position.

6. Minutes of the American Literature Group, Modern Language Association (Univ. of Wisconsin).

7. *Literary History of the United States,* archives (Univ. of Pennsylvania,
Philadelphia). Professor Wilt has graciously given me permission to quote
this letter.

1948

✂ PREFACE TO ✂
LITERARY HISTORY OF THE UNITED STATES

The American literary history movement reached its culmination in November 1948 when LHUS appeared. Although it was widely and variously reviewed in this country and in England, its special position in the history of American thought was not generally appreciated. In Germany, however, and later in Japan and India, when perspectives began to clear, the whole movement was brought into focus by Franz H. Link, Robert Weimann, and Sujit Mukherjee.[1] A similar attempt to survey the entire range of American literary history, *The Literature of the American People,* edited by Arthur Hobson Quinn and others in 1951, further emphasized the climactic nature of this moment.

In order to preserve the feeling of anonymity and to enable the narrative to flow without interruption, the preface and address to the reader were unsigned. I wrote the first and Henry Canby the second. The authorship of the individual chapters was listed at the back of the book, but the chapters themselves were unsigned. The underlying philosophy of literary history was nowhere discussed and the table of contents alone disclosed the design and structure of the narrative. A

---

1. Franz H. Link, *Amerikanische Literaturegeschichtsschreibung, Ein Forschungsbericht* (Stuttgart, 1963). Robert Weimann, "Tradition und Krise Amerikanischer Literarhistorie Zur ihren Methodologie und Geschichte," in *Weimarer Beitrage,* (Berlin, 1965). Sujit Mukherjee, "The Progress of American Literary History," *Indian Essays in American Literature,* (Bombay, 1968), pp. 305-319.

great building is the work of many hands, but it should not
at first reveal the architect's blueprints or the detailed work of
the stonemason, the riveter, and the carpenter.

Each generation should produce at least one literary history of
the United States, for each generation must define the past in its
own terms. A redefinition of our literary past was needed at the
time of the First World War, when the *Cambridge History of American Literature* was produced by a group of scholars. It is now needed
again; and it will be needed still again.

At mid-point, the twentieth century may properly establish its
own criteria of literary judgment; indeed, the values as well as the
facts of modern civilization must be examined if man is to escape
self-destruction. We must know and understand better the recorders
of our experience. Scholars can no longer be content to write for
scholars; they must make their knowledge meaningful and applicable to humanity. As our part of that task, the editors, associates,
and contributors have undertaken and completed this work.

Such a history could be the work of one or a few hands, or it
could be a collaboration of many. But the United States, in its life
of less than two centuries, has produced too much literature for
any one man to read and digest. Its literary history can therefore be
best written by a group of collaborators, whatever the risk of differences of perspective or opinion.

Those who have joined in this undertaking are historians and
critics rather than specialists in a narrow sense. Their contributions
are related to one another within a frame rather than separately
composed essays. Each member of our company has a proportional
share in the whole enterprise rather than an exclusive interest in his
part of it.

The drawing of the design and the assignment of chapters took a
year of conferences in which every point was discussed to a satisfactory conclusion. Seven men took part in this planning: the four
editors and the three associates. Each of the additional forty-eight
contributors had at hand a detailed outline of the entire work and a
statement of basic principles before he agreed to write. Upon his
acceptance, he was asked to meet, either individually or in group
conferences, with the editors and associates and with the authors of

allied chapters, and discuss the problems presented by his assignment. Three years were given to the writing; two more, to the editing
and publishing. During this period each of the three editors who
had undertaken major tasks of detail was granted a year of freedom
from professional duties in order to give full time to the work, and
in some instances contributors received grants-in-aid. All the bibliographical essays were written by one editor in close collaboration
with the authors of relevant chapters.

A genuine collaboration requires some sacrifice of the individual
in the interest of the group. The authorship of each chapter is given
on pp. 1442-1445, but the chapters are unsigned in the text. Many
of them have been substantially revised in order to fit them into
the larger plan, and parts of some have been lifted and incorporated
elsewhere. The editors have themselves written many chapters and
have supplied necessary links; but individual opinions and styles
have not been altered in substance. The result is, they believe, a
coherent narrative, with valuable differences on individual points.
Principles of orthography in quotations have been left to the judgment of the respective contributors.

The almost ideal conditions which made this procedure possible
were created by The Macmillan Company and the Rockefeller
Foundation, with supplementary aid from the American Council
of Learned Societies, the American Philosophical Society, and the
institutions with which several of the editors were connected—
Swarthmore College, Princeton University, the University of Pennsylvania, and the Lawrenceville School. The disruptions of the war
and post-war eras, far from presenting handicaps, have stimulated
interest by emphasizing the need for cultural redefinition.

It would be impossible to make specific acknowledgment of indebtedness to the scholars who indirectly contributed to this work.
In some instances, the debt was immediate and personal, but more
often it took the form of dependence upon the great body of critical,
historical, and analytical studies that the past quarter of a century
has produced. The mere listing of names and books here or in footnotes would be meaningless. The bibliographical essays, which
attempt to be critical both in their selection and in their arrangement
of entries, must serve as confession of obligation on almost every
point. There would be little reason for attempting again the task

which the *Cambridge History* undertook for its generation were it not for the pioneering work of such historians as F. L. Pattee, A. H. Quinn, W. B. Cairns, P. H. Boynton, and V. L. Parrington; the stimulation of scholarship by these and other such teachers as Norman Foerster, J. B. Hubbell, R. L. Rusk, and H. H. Clark; the bibliographical work of E. E. Leisy, Gregory Paine, and their associates; the invigorating perceptions of such critics as W. C. Brownell, John Macy, Stuart P. Sherman, Van Wyck Brooks, and Edmund Wilson; and the specific investigations of a host of careful scholars.

The entire text of this book was prepared specifically for it under individual contracts with contributors for their respective parts of a single over-all plan.

1954

By 1954, LHUS had weathered the storm of reviews in praise and in protest and had been accepted generally as a single definitive work in its field—the true story of American literature. It then seemed time to release a book that I had started to write in 1947 when I was welding the chapters of the big book into a coherent whole and to make explicit the cyclical theory of organic relationship between the work of art and the experience that prompted it. In the context of American history, this theory revealed two cycles, both created by the movement of Western culture from East to West across a wilderness continent. *The Cycle of American Literature,* a pocket guide for the journey, was the result.

There seems now to be little doubt in the minds of critics at home and abroad that the United States has produced, during the twentieth century, a distinctive literature, worthy to take its place with the great literatures of other times and other peoples. There is no similar agreement on the reasons for this, or for the apparently sudden cultural maturity of a people which, throughout nearly two centuries of political independence, has thought of itself as heterogeneous and derivative in its racial and cultural make-up. American writings of the past quarter-century give evidence of a literary renaissance which could come only from a long tradition and a united culture. This literary renaissance, the second to occur in the United States, must have both a history and a pattern of relationships within itself. As yet it has not been clearly defined or understood, because literary historians have failed to comprehend it as an organic whole.

The theory of literary history which was most generally held during the nineteenth century proposed that, because almost all of the literature produced by citizens of the United States was written in the English language, and because literature is expression and can presumably be best described by the language in which it is expressed, American literature is, and always will be, a branch of English literature. The consequence of this theory was that undue emphasis was placed on the Colonial period, on that part of the United States which most successfully preserved its British characteristics, New England, and on those authors, like Irving, Longfellow, Lowell, and Howells, who discovered ways of using American "materials" without greatly violating British proprieties. Writers like Walt Whitman, Herman Melville, Mark Twain, and Theodore Dreiser, who were more deeply American than any of the other group, were dismissed either as evidences of a cruder stage in cultural development or as curiosities. Thus an American romantic movement could be clearly distinguished as evolving from the imitative beginnings of Irving, Cooper, and Bryant, and culminating in the poetry of the bearded sages of the Cambridge group. Thereafter came the "Gilded Age," a deterioration into "realism" and "pessimism," and a literature in the twentieth century that was described as close to degenerate in both inspiration and form. Literary histories which are firmly rooted in this misleading theory are still produced and sold by the thousands of copies in the United States and elsewhere.

The first successful challenge to this theory—not counting the pioneer work of Moses Coit Tyler—came in 1927 with V. L. Parrington's *Main Currents in American Thought,* the literary historian's version of a widespread movement in historical writing which was then attempting to retell the record of the past in terms of economic and other forms of environmental determinism. The literary historian of this school owed his ultimate debt to Taine, Hegel, and Marx, but as an American and a democrat he recognized the social philosophies of none of these masters, taking from them only the method of relating literary expression directly and simply to the life which it expressed. American schools began to use "Literature and Life" readers instead of the old "Belles-Lettres" varieties, while scholars in the universities and journalists outside began a process of reevaluation of both major and minor American authors and their works. The result was a new pattern of American literary history that succeeded in rediscovering such writers as Freneau, Thoreau, and Melville; in giving more sympathetic recognition to Whitman and Mark Twain; in showing just what was American in such writers as Henry James; and in arousing widespread interest in humor, local color, realism, folk ballads and legends, and in minor authors who were faithful to their materials and reflected the ideas and moods of their times. Under this dispensation the literature of the late nineteenth century and of the years that followed could at least be regarded without prejudice, and awarded laurels for its vigor and its authenticity, even though at times it seemed to lose its character as art.

The pendulum had again swung too far. So great was the value assigned, under this theory, to accuracy of record that the best literature seemed to be merely that which stuck closest to the facts. Imagination was crowded aside by political and social data, and American literary history threatened to become no more than a history of documentation; often, as even in the case of Parrington, the documentation of a specific theory of social and political development. Ironically, major authors like Poe, Dickinson, and Henry James, who in one way or another were above or outside the obvious data of American life, seemed irrelevant and alien, at the same time that others, like Cooper, Melville, and Mark Twain, were gaining a new dimension. Although this theory made possible an American literary history, it threatened to make literary history as such an anomaly. In its most extreme form it even accepted the Marxian formula and imposed a schematic dogma that was not too different from the "socialist realism" of the dictatorships.

An escape into pure aesthetic analysis, which many critics then proposed, was not the resolution of this dilemma. It was rather an acknowledgment of failure by the literary historian, a confession that he had lost faith in the continuity of life and the organic principle of its expression in art. There was no good reason why, with the old prejudices cleared away and the relationship between American literature and American life clearly established, the real literary history of the United States could not begin to take shape.

The writer of this new history must first recognize that the major author, even though he becomes major by rising above his times or otherwise alienating himself from his society, is nevertheless the specific product of his times and of his society, and probably their most profound expression. Literature, therefore, has a relationship to social and intellectual history, not as documentation, but as symbolic illumination. Valid literary history must concern itself chiefly with major authors, but it must deal with them, both directly and indirectly, in provable context. Therefore the first task of the American literary historian was to discover which were or are the major American authors, and not to be misled by the fact that some of them denied their country and became expatriates, others lashed out against it with satire or overt denunciations, or escaped from it into dreams and fantasies. These are merely varying forms of relationship between the writer and his materials.

The rational view of history, which deals only with logical sequences of cause and effect, is inadequate to deal with relationships such as these. If there is one idea that most major American authors have in common, it is the belief that life is organic; and the American literary historian can do no better than to adopt for his study an organic view of history. The individual organism follows the circular pattern of life; it has beginning, a life cycle, and an end. This simple principle may be discovered in the structure of a poem, in the biography of an author, in the rise and fall of a local or particular cultural movement, or in the over-all evolution of a national literature. The historian's task is to discover the cycle, or cycles, by which his literature is determined both in general scheme and in detail. American literature, when reviewed in terms of its major authors and from the vantage point of the period of its greatest achievement, the twentieth century, reveals such a cyclic rhythm.

The basic theme for this rhythm is also the central historical fact of the American experiment: the removal of a mature and sophisticated civilization—that of Western Europe—to a primitive continent ideally suited to its needs and virtually unexploited of its apparently infinite natural resources. The American expansion to the West, and the impact in turn of the newly formed civilization on its parent, set the circular pattern for the whole story. On the level of symbolic illumination, the literary historian must disclose the vast and intricate pattern of this unfolding cycle, perhaps not yet completed, but firmly defined by its varied recurrences through four centuries.

When applied to the story of American literature as a whole, this cyclic theory discloses not only a single organic movement, but at least two secondary cycles as well: the literary movement which developed from the Eastern seaboard as a center, and culminated with the great romantic writers of the mid-nineteenth century; and that which grew out of the conquest of the continent and is now rounding its full cycle in the twentieth century. When applied to the individual work, the same theory supplies a formula for measuring the aesthetic distance of a poem or play or novel from its origins in some phase of American experience. The letter home comes first, then the debate on religion or philosophy, then the imitative work of art, and finally the original and organic expression of the new life. Thus the process of cultural growth into art is endlessly repeated as a civilization moves forward in time.

The historian of this process, on the other hand, takes his position in the present and looks backward over the past. His is the task of reorganizing experience so that its larger meanings are revealed, rather than that of repeating history in all its details. He must select, omit, and reorganize from the great mass of available data so that a coherent view of the total literary culture can emerge. The broad contours of a landscape and the organic pattern of its hills and valleys can be seen only from a height at which some details are obscured and others take on meaningful relationships because of the angle of vision of the observer. The writing of history, like other forms of art, requires aesthetic distance before it can claim perspective.

This book is an essay toward such a singleness of vision. It is also and inescapably a by-product of the shared experience of editing the *Literary History of the United States.* Ideas and methods which in that project could be used only as implements of organization can here take full control because one person alone is responsible for them. The editors and contributors of that ambitious work need not be implicated in the methods and conclusions of this lesser one by a simple acknowledgment of so long and intimate an association. That several of them cared enough to read this manuscript with keen and helpful advice—in particular, Willard Thorp, Thomas H. Johnson, and Sculley Bradley—does not lessen the debt. The manuscript also owes much to the scrutiny of my wife, Mary S. Spiller, and of Thomas J. Johnston, Sigmund Skard and other friends who read all or parts of it.

✖ A LETTER TO ✖
AMERICAN LITERARY HISTORIANS

In 1958-1959 when I was visiting professor at the University of London, I learned that the annual meeting of the American Literature Group of the Modern Language Association was again to be devoted to the old question of how to prepare for the time when, in its turn, LHUS would presumably be obsolete and a new kind of literary history might evolve for a new generation. I was not invited to comment, but our interests were so very much at stake that I could not resist writing a letter to the chairman, Walter Blair of the University of Chicago, which he read at the luncheon. No action was taken at that time.

I have been so closely associated with the activities of the American Literature Group in literary history and bibliography since the 1920's that I cannot refrain from expressing my pleasure at this new spurt of interest and energy in the perennial reinterpretation of our literary past. Not only must each generation write its own literary history, as the editors of the 1948 *Literary History of the United States* assumed, but each group and each individual who develops a hypothesis and a method must be allowed to make his own contribution in his own way; for the writing of history is never done as long as anyone can read new meanings into his own life by studying the reflection of the present in the mirror of the past. As long as we are vitally concerned with the problems of the relationship of the now to the then, the work of art to the artist, and literature to its society, our historical scholarship will be alive; as soon as we feel that we have answered all such questions, we will become moribund. The danger in a work like *The Cambridge History of American Literature* or the *Literary History of the United States,* or any massive synthesis, is that it can act as a deterrent to intellectual curiosity by giving a false sense of a false finality. Of the making of histories there is no end, and much scholarship of the right kind is the very lifeblood of a culture.

As I look back on the movement which, from my point of view at least, culminated in the *Literary History of the United States,* I see it as the scholarly part of the so-called renaissance of the second and third decades of this century. America's cultural "coming-of-age" in that era is now a generally accepted historical fact. The completion of the historical process which established one of the modern world powers on this North American continent and gave it full political, economic, and intellectual self-awareness found expression, in the years 1912 to 1920, in the poetry, fiction, and criticism of a major group of writers. The same movement brought a new crop of literary histories by Quinn, Boynton, Cairns, Van Doren, Foerster, and Parrington to assert a vigorous nationalism instead of the lingering colonialism of our then elder statesmen. Strongly influenced by the economic determinism and the intellectual challenge of the "new" history, they stressed the social and philosophical contexts of American writings in order to establish firmly the integration of our literary past with the forces which had shaped our civilization.

The *Literary History of the United States* attempted to sum up the achievement and point of view of this generation of scholars, but it also challenged their limitations in three important ways: by a series of "instrument" chapters, by emphasis on the masterwork and the major writer, and by examining the relationships of American to European as well as to English literatures and cultures.

In the "instrument" chapters it related the work of art to the factors of environment which immediately conditioned it—the processes in the making and the consumption of the literary product per se. In so doing, it raised in specific terms that could be understood by the social scientists the problems of the direct relationship of literature to the culture of which it is a major expression. Even now, this kind of sociology of literature is still in its infancy, but at least we understand better than we did in 1940 just how the presence or absence of publishers, periodicals, copyright laws, circulating libraries, booksellers, educational institutions, theatres, and other such agencies are essentials of the form and direction of any literary development.

At the other extreme, the *Literary History of the United States* proposed that the meaning of a national literature can best be sought in its masterworks and its major authors rather than in the clusters of minor and subliterary productions which are the delight of the social or intellectual historian. Selecting somewhat arbitrarily the authors and books which our generation had come to agree upon as our highest literary achievements, it discovered two peaks of performance in the periods 1835-1855 and 1915-1935, and it then subordinated all other aspects of the history to the task of explaining and evaluating the cultural processes which thus culminated. By pointing to the need for fresh study of the really important literary works and authors in themselves as well as in their contexts, it suggested a kind of analytical and evaluative criticism at that time none too common among us.

It is in these two respects that the *Literary History of the United States* predicted the two major trends in our scholarship of the past two decades. The new criticism (I do not use the term in a special sense) has sharpened the tools of analysis and has discovered in the psychology of the work of art and of the creative process new and important bases for aesthetic understanding. By turning attention from the causes of literary production to the results in the literary product itself, a whole generation of critics has taught us how to write the chapters on masterworks and major authors around which the architecture of the next literary history must be constructed.

On the other hand, the American studies movement (again, I use the term in a general sense) has taught us that a culture is to be discovered as much in the composite imagination of a people as in their habits of economic and political behavior. Largely with the help of the cultural anthropologists, the social scientists of the present are beginning to study mature and sophisticated cultures as configurations of social consent, habit, and communal expression in much the same way that primitive societies have been so successfully interpreted. Again, we have barely made a start in developing the needed methods for this kind of study, but it is surely here that the literary historians of the future will find the mortar with which to weld the bricks of their aesthetic analyses of masterworks into the story of the historical development of our national culture.

A third respect in which the *Literary History of the United States* opened doors which have subsequently been widened was in calling attention to the increasing interdependence of American and European literatures and cultures. Some historical critics today even go so far as to say that national and racial factors are no longer of importance in the modern world of swift and easy intercommunication—that what we need is a history of modern rather than of American literature. They may be right, for it is increasingly difficult to assign nationality to such writers as Joyce, Proust, Kafka, Eliot, Auden, and Pasternak, but such a view tends to forget the breakup of the vast colonial empires of the nineteenth century and the simultaneous growth of local, racial, and national movements toward self-determination which are now apparent in all parts of the world. This is not the place to discuss so broad and so controversial a problem, but I would like to conclude by expressing the view that the new literary history must retain a sense of the autonomy of the immediate cultural context of every work of art if it is to be history at all. There is no historical continuity in art as such. Masterworks are related to masterworks in a realm that knows no time or place. For the historian even the great work of art is the expression of a culture at a specific moment in its development, and only in the progress of human society will he discover the process which culminates from time to time in supreme aesthetic fulfillment.

If another literary history is needed for another time, it will not result from the anti-historicism of some of our literary critics or from the anti-aestheticism which has infected some of our social scientists. It will come rather from those who have learned to use judiciously the insights and the methods of both the analytical critics and the behavioral scientists and who can apply the findings of both groups to the task of telling once again what our literary achievement really is and how it came to be what it is.

1976

LITERARY HISTORY AND LITERARY CRITICISM

Since 1958 there have appeared many special studies in historical criticism and factual research that have corrected the record and deepened the understanding of our national literary story, but no new comprehensive literary history of the United States has as yet appeared, although there have been several announcements of such projects, and a number of short histories of periods, types, and themes have been published. The most influential of these, *Virgin Land* by Henry Nash Smith, identified the frontier with the myth of the "Garden" and gave rise to similar works on American "Innocence," the "Fortunate Fall," the "Machine in the Garden," "regeneration through violence," and other efforts to write literary history around an American mythology. More recently, phenomenology and structuralism have suggested that there is continuity in the history of an American language or "style," colloquial or otherwise, but they too end by being essays in historical criticism, which give density to literary history without providing a historical philophy and structure sound and comprehensive enough to contain the whole story. It would seem, therefore, that the socio-aesthetic philosophy and the evolutionary structure posited by the editorial board of *Literary History of the United States* are as valid now as they were in 1948.

INDEX